Meet Me at the Palaver

Meet Me at the Palaver

*Narrative Pastoral Counseling
in Postcolonial Contexts*

TAPIWA N. MUCHERERA

CASCADE *Books* · Eugene, Oregon

MEET ME AT THE PALAVER
Narrative Pastoral Counseling in Postcolonial Contexts

Cascade Books
A Division of Wipf and Stock Publishers
199 W. 8th Ave., Suite 3
Eugene, OR 97401

www.wipfandstock.com

ISBN 13: 978-1-55635-971-2

Cataloging-in-Publication data:

Mucherera, Tapiwa N.

Meet me at the palaver : narrative pastoral counseling in postcolonial contexts / Tapiwa N. Mucherera.

x + 142 p. ; 23 cm. —Includes bibliographical references.

ISBN 13: 978-1-55635-971-2

1. Pastoral counseling—Zimbabwe. 2. Shona—Pastoral counseling. I. Title.

BV4012.2 .M833 2009

Manufactured in the U.S.A.

Contents

Acknowledgments vii
Preface ix

1 Introduction: Remembering Our History, and Forging Stories of a Hopeful Future 1

2 Clashing Cultures and Ethical Values in the Age of HIV/AIDS 27

3 A Culture of Death: Poverty and HIV/AIDS 56

4 Signposts of Hope: Religion, Revillaging, and Reauthoring 76

5 The Palaver and Beyond: A Holistic Narrative Pastoral Care and Counseling Approach 99

Bibliography 135

Acknowledgments

IN MY ACADEMIC journey, many teachers and conversation partners have influenced my thinking in terms of pastoral theology and counseling. Many thanks to Drs. P. U. M. Mlambo, Edward Wimberly, Larry Graham, Joretta Marshall, Ann Gatobu, Emmanuel Lartey, Archie Smith, to the late Masamba Mpolo and Michael White—to name a few. Outside the field of pastoral counseling, Drs. Gwinyai H. Muzorewa, George Tinker, Teresia Hinga, Ngugi wa Thiong'o, Musa Dube, Isabel Phiri, and Art Jones, have contributed to or challenged my thoughts. Special thanks to Rev. Geoffrey Kagoro for the time we spent together reflecting on the issues of poverty and the HIV/AIDS situation in Africa, and particularly in Zimbabwe. Many times, you raised questions that needed further reflection to sharpen my thoughts.

This work could not have been accomplished without the help of those who volunteered to be interviewed. I want to thank Mai Tsikai for allowing me to have access to those with whom you worked who were HIV/AIDS infected, and whose stories could have died with them but are now in print. Their stories will continue and hopefully will give others hope and wisdom.

Rev. Mwandira and Mai Musuka, the trips we took around Zimbabwe to different orphanages and communities to establish grinding-mill projects added much to this work. I hope others will learn from what is written to establish similar projects to support the orphans and the widows around the world. Thanks to my friends at Mount Zion United Methodist Church in Kentucky, and at St. Luke's United Methodist Church Highlands, Colorado—and more specifically Rev. Dr. Thobaben and Laurie Gilbert for your unwavering support in the funding of the orphan projects to care for the "least of these."

The late bishop Christopher Jokomo at one time told me that I might not get enough support needed for these projects, or that I might even be ridiculed—but to never give up on the vision. He reminded me that to give up because of being ridiculed would be giving up on the widows and orphans; rather I was to focus on this holistic vision of caring for the widows and orphans through these projects.

I thank my mother, Tracy, and my late father, Nicodimus Gandidzwana, for believing in me and being able to acknowledge the gifts and graces God gave me. I was able to produce this book based on the values you instilled in me of caring for the needy. Growing up, I don't remember a day we ever lived only as a nuclear family. It seemed there was always someone in need in our home, and you always gratefully took each one into your care. You taught us to have a heart for the needy, and through your actions I learned what it means to sacrifice for the sake of others. My mother's caring continues today, especially with her concerns for those affected and infected by HIV/AIDS. Thanks to my late auntie, Naomi Mundondo, and grandmother, Chemunoisa, who both had gifts as storytellers. Now some of the stories and words of wisdom they shared with me live on in print.

Thanks to my wife, Bertha, and my children, Shamiso, Anesu, and Ruvimbo, for every little bit of support and hugs you gave me throughout. Auntie Virginia, Simba, Kuda, and Nyasha Kagoro, thanks for those moments we spent together reflecting and praying for the needy, especially the orphans of Zimbabwe—we will continue to do so.

Cheri Cowell, thanks for your tirelessness in helping me with the final editing of this work for submission to the publisher. Your feedback was marvelous and very much appreciated. Jeremy Funk, my copy editor, you are blessed with a keen eye. I appreciated working with you in the final editing of this manuscript. Claire Williams, thanks for some of the typing you did for me. Thanks to everyone else whom I might have overlooked.

Ultimately, glory, honor and thanks be to God, through Christ and the Holy Spirit, who gave me the strength and wisdom to put this project together. Thanks to the Lord Almighty, whose love and justice for widows and orphans never ceases!

Preface

THIS BOOK IS an attempt to present an indigenous *holistic, narrative pastoral counseling* approach in postcolonial indigenous contexts, with a focus on Zimbabwe. It opens with a history and stories of change brought about by colonialism and Christianity to indigenous contexts such as Zimbabwe, and an examination of how colonization subjugated and marginalized the culture, values, religion, and the humanity of African peoples. Narrative pastoral counseling has always been present in indigenous contexts, since story is the way of life. Problems are shared in family, community, or group settings called the "palaver." A palaver (*padare*) is an informal gathering usually for the purposes of providing counsel and support for those facing personal, family, and/or community crisis and problems, and sometimes for the purposes of education and to share joys.[1] In most cases, the problems, education, or joys are shared in the form of stories.

In this book, I argue that therapy or counseling as taught in the West will not always suffice in indigenous contexts since these theories tend to promote and focus on individuality, autonomy, and independence. The training of counselors in indigenous contexts needs encourage counselors who will "get off their couch or chair" and into the neighborhood. The type of counselor needed in these contexts is one trained to essentially work with orphans and widows using a *holistic, narrative pastoral counseling approach* in assessing and servicing the three basic areas of human needs: *the body, mind, and spirit*. This counselor would need to have the skills of a social worker as well as well as those of a counselor.

---

1. In Zimbabwe, the Shona word for "palaver" is *padare* or *kudare*. A palaver can occur in many different forms. It can happen at family, extended-family, and community levels as a formal or informal gathering (open or closed) to resolve a crisis or a problem, or at times just to meet. Traditionally it was led by a family elder or community chief; however, everyone who sits at the palaver has a voice.

Christianity brought the Bible, and today people are able to weave together biblical stories with the traditional folktales, metaphors, and symbols in narrating their life stories. Folklores, using animals as players, allow room for those telling their story to externalize their problems, thus giving one an opportunity to attack the problem head-on. In this way, the problem is externalized from the person to the symbolic animal character, giving the person room to step back and analyze the problem without feeling blamed. Narrative pastoral counseling uses naming and externalizing processes in speaking the unspeakable. How can we, for example, address the HIV/AIDS crisis—a crisis requiring an open discussion about sex, itself a topic not usually talked about in public? The palaver is the answer. The issues of poverty, poor medical systems, and inclusion of such Western ethical standards as confidentiality have complicated the ways in which indigenous contexts address problems such as the HIV/AIDS pandemic.

In addition, how can we move away from some of our traditional values that may threaten the widows and young girls in some of these indigenous contexts? Must a young widow be forced into a marriage inheritance to a man known to have lost his wife to HIV/AIDS, because it is the *customary thing to do*? Though no longer at the center of today's indigenous societies (especially in the cities), the traditional palaver healing/counseling process has not been totally lost *and* can be easily reclaimed.

African people have always depended on God and the neighbor. Revillaging, religion, and reauthoring are the main signposts for the future in these contexts faced with horrendous suffering from poverty and HIV/AIDS. Today scholars and other writers from indigenous contexts are being called upon to reauthor the subjugated history of the past, bringing it from the margins to the center. The blending of the past and the present can be one way to bring a hopeful future. The church palaver as exemplified in this book can help foster that hopeful future.

1

Introduction

*Remembering Our History, and Forging
Stories of a Hopeful Future*

"Mudzimu weshiri uri mudendere."
("The ancestry, roots, and survival of a bird are in its nest.")

—Shona proverb

"Usakanganwe chezuro ngehope" literally translates from Shona to mean, "Do not forget yesterday's experiences because of a good night's sleep." Even in situations where one experiences a bad night, one does not forget other past experiences because of the night experience. A common saying among the Shona is, "When you forget your past, you will never know the truth." For how can we know where we are going if we don't know where we've come from or where we are presently located? When one loses the memories of one's past, one is most likely to lose one's present grounding, and ultimately one's place of embeddedness in the future as well.

History is a contextual story. People create history out of stories rooted in their ancestry. Past stories, when weaved together with narratives from modern indigenous communities, contribute to the constructing or forming of both individual and communal identities. This chapter serves both as an introduction to the accounts of a common encounter of the indigenous peoples (colonization and Christianity) and as an introduction to the whole book (how the past and the present narratives of indigenous Africans can be woven together to create a hopeful future using narrative pastoral counseling). This book is about how narrative pastoral counseling—or how stories (personal, family, community, folk, biblical)—can be used in pastoral care and counseling to restore hope in contemporary indigenous communities such as Zimbabwe, despite stories of subjugation from the past, and in light of the present context of the HIV and AIDS pandemic, poverty, and other problems. The palaver (*pachiara, padare*), a traditional narrative-counseling approach common in many traditional indigenous settings and still present in many African contexts, will also be explored for how it could be reintroduced in most of today's African contexts.[1] As much as this book focuses on Africa, and more specifically on the Shona of Zimbabwe, the material it covers can be easily generalized to many of the indigenous contexts that experienced colonialism and who are faced with poverty and the HIV/AIDS pandemic. In order to understand the indigenous people's story, one cannot ignore a people's past historical experiences, since these still have great impact on the people today. Thus this book presents their struggles, and in the last chapters closes with how hope can be restored in such contexts as Zimbabwe. Finally, the work of African churches and communities will be highlighted—these beacons bringing hope to the grim context of poverty and the HIV/AIDS pandemic.

Indigenous People: A History in Synopsis

The contexts and life narratives of indigenous peoples have been a "mixed bag," given that indigenous people have been viewed both as blessed and as the "wretched of the earth"[2] due to imperialism. They are blessed in that these contexts have persevered and preserved a rich source of humanity's traditional religiocultural values. Still today anthropologists study these communities to understand the origins of humanity's traditional wisdom and ways of life. In most of these contexts where there was and is less "invasion," they are still rich in natural resources and uncharted lands.

1. The palaver, a narrative counseling approach, used in indigenous contexts and common in traditional Africa and more specifically in Zimbabwe, will be introduced in later chapters. Details about the setting, purpose, and processes of palaver will be addressed later from a narrative pastoral counseling perspective.

2. Fanon, *Wretched of the Earth.*

One of the root causes of the "wretchedness" of indigenous peoples came by way of subjugation through colonial imperialism. These stories are filled with pain and suffering. Today suffering continues under neocolonial governments, unjust economic structures (locally and globally), and the pandemic diseases, such as HIV and AIDS. However, these experiences of pain and suffering have not totally eroded the hope for a better future.

Survival is the dominant story one hears even in these desperate situations. As the old adage states, "In times of drought, the survival of a tree is in the depth of its roots." History has taught indigenous people that there is always hope if they are rooted in God and remember that God always raises a "stump, the holy seed" (Isa 6:13). In these difficult situations, stories from precolonial and colonial times are shared, reminding the younger generation not to focus only on the painful neocolonial present, but to also imagine what the future would and will look like. Even under this inescapable net of neocolonialism, hope is found as indigenous people groups seek to remember the story of who they are as a people, and as they focus on alternative possibilities to the present story.

> Surely, Simba, one of the strongest and wisest lions, knew who he was. But hunters, still searching for the extent of their boundaries, came to capture and dominate Simba. With guns aimed, they engulfed the lion in a large net made of complex systems of knots, the likes of which Simba had never before experienced. The hunters kept Simba trapped under the net for a very long time, all the while working to convince the great lion that he was no longer strong, that he was no longer wise. But Simba remembered his Father's stories of how fast a younger Simba was able to run and how deep his sharp teeth could cut. Simba longed to run free again, and so he began using his teeth to gnaw through the captors' net, bit by bit, until he was free. One big roar and the captors ran away. Simba stretched his muscles and rose up, but he found that he was not altogether free yet, for he had forgotten how to act as a free lion he had once been. He asked himself, "Who is Simba? Where is his home? What is Simba to be doing?" What will become of Simba? It took Simba time to remember what it meant to be a strong and wise lion of Africa. He had to walk the path he had once trod, but it was no longer the same. The path he had walked before his capture was now thick with mounds of grass. To take the same path the

hunters had followed seemed foolish. Simba would have to create a new path and a new future.[3]

Much change has taken place in the religiocultural and psychological worldview of neocolonial indigenous nations, and more specifically in Africa, since the advent of Christianity and colonialism. Three
different layers of stories exist in the African context: the precolonial or
traditional, the colonial, and the post- or neocolonial stories. All three
levels are important in addressing situations of narrative pastoral crisis
intervention or counseling. The stories of precolonial or traditional
times still form some of the foundations and are highly influential for
indigenous people around the world. As much as the histories of most
indigenous people were passed down orally, one cannot ignore this part
of their story and expect to fully understand them.

The arrival of the colonialists marked the start of written history,
since in these contexts history was passed down orally. Colonial history writers did not bother to include the oral history of the indigenous peoples. Written history, therefore, in most indigenous contexts
was written or presented to the exclusion of precolonial eras. Some
Westerners regard the stories of the indigenous people as an unnecessary inconvenience. It is as if they are saying, "If we could just rid them
of their precolonial history and educate all the indigenous people to a
Western way of life, then this world would be a better place." A joke is
usually shared about a colonizer who said: "Our country [the colonized
country] would be a better place without you natives." The colonizers
forgot they were the foreigners. Besides distorting historical facts, another violation the colonists committed was taking native lands.

The Subjugation of Natives' Land through Violence

From indigenous people colonizers stole land—one of the greatest resources, which native peoples held dear. The natives did not believe in
owning the land, but instead saw it as a gift from the Creator. The land
was guarded by the "living dead," or ancestors, in order to feed the living. Of the Shona belief about the land Bourdillon says:

---

3. The story of Simba the lion is unpublished, written by Sharon Hayes of Wilmore,
Kentucky, for the cross-cultural class I taught at Asbury Theological Seminary in
January 2004.

'Ownership' of the land by the spirits is bound up with the relationship between the spirits and the living community. The
land forms a close and enduring bond between the living and
the dead—through their control of the fertility of the land they
once cultivated, the spirits are believed to continue to care for
their descendants and the descendants are forced to remember and honor their ancestors. . . . The association between the
spirits and the land is expressed in the tradition of *chisi*, days
sacred to the spirits, on which people should not work the soil
in any way.[4]

The earth is not "dirt" as it is referred to in the West, but was and
still is the source of life. It is a generally held belief by most indigenous
peoples that they were created out of "mother earth—the soil," and from
her they receive nourishment, livelihood, and their sustenance. When
colonizers came, they did not live by these same values. Land, and all
that was on it, was to be subdued and plundered for personal gain.
The colonizers took the hospitality of the natives as stupidity. Musa W.
Dube, a professor at the University of Botswana, relates the common
story that she quotes from Mofokeng's article on how the Africans lost
their land in exchange for the Bible. Dube writes:

The story is held that 'when the white man came to our country
he had the Bible and we had the land. The white man said to us,
'let us pray.' After the prayer, the white man had the land and we
had the Bible.' The story summarizes the sub-Saharan experience of colonization. It explains how colonization was connected to the coming of the white man, how it was connected to the
use of the Bible, and how the black African's possession of the
Bible is connected to the white man's taking of African people's
lands. Admittedly, the story holds that the Bible is now a sub-
Saharan African book, but it is an inheritance that will always,
in the mind of the African, be linked to and remembered for its
role in facilitating European imperialism.[5]

Being stripped of their land was one of the most painful experiences of the natives. To add to the agony of losing their land, the whites,
who had been offered land to settle, turned around and at gunpoint
drove the natives from the most fertile lands to the barren areas of the
country. Doris Lessing (winner of the Nobel Prize in Literature in 2007),

4. Bourdillon, *Shona Peoples*, 70.
5. Dube, *Postcolonial Feminist Interpretation of the Bible*, 3.

a well-known British writer deported from then-Rhodesia for opposing the white government, writes about when she was a young white witnessing her parents buy land from the government—land from which the natives had been moved:

> My parents bought from the government for a few shillings an acre, land off which the Africans had been moved to free it for 'white development.' That is, the Africans whose land it was were forcibly moved off it—by physical violence. This is not how white people who 'settled' the country saw the process. They saw themselves as 'civilized' (being white), while the black people were savage, and indeed benefiting from contact with these superior beings. The Africans were put into Native Reserves. The Natives Reserves of Rhodesia, like of those of South Africa, had, and have, the poorest soil, the least water, and the worst of everything, from roads to shops.[6]

The land-grabbing issue was one of the major causes of some of the uprisings that followed. The wars that Africans fought against white settlers were mainly due to Africans' losing their land. Michael F. C. Bourdillon, a white ethnographer and former professor at the University of Zimbabwe, also recognizes that many Shona people were moved from their rich lands to barren "tribal lands," and that in some parts of the country the whites did not cause any problems for the natives because some of the areas were barren from the beginning. He says:

> Many tribal areas are situated in rocky and hilly country with shallow sandy soils covering the sparsely arable land. In some places, people were originally moved off better land to make way for white farmers and resettled in the less arable country of neighboring chiefdoms. In certain other areas, people are aware that they were left in peace because their land was too poor for white use. In those areas where more fertile, heavy loams were originally avoided because they were less suited to millet and sorghum, people are now confined for their modern crops to the less fertile soft sands.[7]

This devastated many Africans who were forcibly moved. The connection to land offers more than resources for food production. Land was and is treated with respect, and the connection of people to

6. Lessing, Foreword, xiv.

7. Bourdillon, *Shona Peoples*, 76.

particular places has, for many generations, given them a sense of being "home." Being removed forcibly also took away that familiarity.

The Subjugation and Objectification of African Humanness

The advent of colonialism and Christianity to indigenous contexts was a blending of the coming of "good news" (the Bible) with some of Africans' most horrendous experiences. A publishers' foreword to Bishop Dodge's book begins:

> If you think there is nothing wrong with Christian missions, you should not read this book. But if you happen to be one of those who still think the missionary effort can win if we have the good sense and courage to correct what is wrong and make a new start with what is right, you better read it. . . . [Bishop Dodge] speaks with authority. He knows at firsthand what is and has been wrong, and what he has to say about that has never been said in such language before; it is not conducive to complacency or a good night's sleep, but it happens to be true.[8]

In the same book Bishop Dodge rightly assesses the situation and the activities of the early missionaries to indigenous contexts (and particularly to Africa), and what needs to change:

> The modern missionary must bear the brunt of criticism and for the shortsightedness of his predecessors. . . . Because missionaries came to Africa with more possessions, more education, and more experience than the African colleagues, they were placed on pedestals. . . . They have perpetuated their privileged status, and been aided and abetted by colonial administrators. Too often, both have shared a desire to perpetuate their common position as the "elite" of the society. In many instances, programs of church expansion and missionary activity have been motivated by an attitude of superiority.[9]

The impact of colonialism and Christianity cannot be ignored in how it still affects the African context today. The colonizers and some of the missionaries did not view the indigenous peoples as worthy human beings. Africans were uncultured, and more like the animals. In other words, they looked like humans, but they were more animal-like

8. Dodge, *Unpopular Missionary*, 7.
9. Ibid., 23–24.

than they were human. Some of the colonialists' goals were to kill everything African within the African person and create a new African being, modeled after the European. Lucien Levy-Bruhl, one of the early anthropologist researchers working with missionaries in the African context, said the following about indigenous peoples in intercultural contexts:

> The essential difference between these "savages" and the unbelievers (who are more civilized), is not the result of an intellectual inferiority peculiar to them, it is an actual state, which, according to the Jesuit fathers, is explained by their social condition and their customs. . . . It is extremely difficult to adequately conceive the extent of the ignorance, even of their wise men, on subjects with which infants are conversant in this country. . . . Our friends in Europe would certainly regard the examples we could give of the mental sluggishness of these people in thinking, grasping, and retaining, as absolutely incredible. Even I, who have known them for so long, cannot help being surprised when I see how tremendously difficult it is for them to lay hold of the simplest truths, and above all, to reason anything out for themselves and also how quickly they forget what they have taken in.[10]

In other words, adult primitives were to be treated as infants in terms of thought processes, since they lacked any intellectual quality. Levy-Bruhl goes on to argue that primitive people do not want to think, and are not interested in logic. He further states that missionaries who have studied the natives have also come to the same conclusions that the "primitives never thought and never wanted to think," other than about things necessary to their subsistence living.[11] One of the well-known early missionary writers says about his perception of indigenous/intercultural people and their religion:

> My own view is that savage religion is something not so much thought out as danced out, that in other words, it develops under conditions, psychological and sociological, which favor emotional and motor processes, whereas ideation remains relatively in abeyance.[12]

10. Levy-Bruhl, *Primitive Mentality*, 23, 25.

11. Ibid., 30.

12. Marett, *Threshold of Religion*, xxxi.

Traditional religiocultural systems foundational to some of the traditional religiocultural processes were therefore replaced by new Western scientific cultural worldviews and placed alongside Christian rituals and beliefs. The African who followed the "new religion" was first taken to mission stations to be educated about the ways of the European and then later taught about Christianity.

Some of the missionaries and the colonizers believed that the best way to "save the savages" was educating them by Western superior methods and introducing them to the new religion of Christianity. One of the mistakes these early missionaries and colonizers made was their not realizing that the new religion they were imposing was not a "pure Christianity," but one that was interwoven with their European culture. In many cases, the indigenous peoples were taught the ways of the colonizers before the Bible was introduced to them.

History and past experiences of indigenous peoples form a foundation for their way of life today. Understanding the impact of colonization and Christianity can never be overemphasized. One would not want to underestimate the impact of the above-mentioned attitudes of the colonizers and some of the missionaries as just a thing of the past, without understanding the psychological impact these attitudes have today on those living in these contexts. It is interesting that the methods that colonizers and some missionaries used to deal with indigenous people (and the ways that colonizers and missionaries treated indigenous people) around the world were similar regardless of the indigenous tribe, geography, or race. I agree with George Tinker, a Native American professor, and what he says about the impact of colonization and Christianity on the intercultural contexts of North America in the past and today:

> Psychologically, both at the level of the individual and communally, American Indian people have so internalized the missionary critique of Indian culture and religious traditions, and so internalized our own concession to the superiority of Euroamerican social structures, that we have become complicit in our own oppression. Today, an Indian pastor is more likely than the white missionary to criticize the paganism of traditional spirituality. . . . too many Indian leaders have likewise become stuck in the affirmation of white power and white structures,

even to the point of strongly articulating self-criticism of traditional culture.[13]

As Tinker notes, the impact of colonization and Christianity can be seen today in some of the pastors who give the harshest critiques of their own traditional spiritualities, religion, and way of life as being backward and heathen. Others favor the Western structures over traditional ones, since the traditional ways are perceived as backward.

The Psychological Subjugation and Oppression

There are some indigenous people who believe their local stories do not matter, and that a person who should be regarded as "knowledgeable" is one who has mastered English with a European accent, and Western history, at the expense of any traditional knowledge. Even in today's context, some people still psychologically give more respect to whites than to Africans. By way of an example, a friend of mine, Rev. Christopher Chikoore, and I were on our way to a revival meeting in Zimbabwe, and since we were running late, we decided to buy sandwich fixings. We got into one of two lines to order the cold cuts. When it was just about our turn to order, a white woman walked in but did not stand in either of the two lines as everybody else was; rather she started her own line next to us. The clerk who was serving our line, a Shona woman, then moved from our line to serve the white woman. My friend Chris was riled. The manager heard the commotion, came out, heard what had happened, and apologized to us as he served our line. Then, as they say, "what goes around comes around." The white woman did not like the way her meats had been cut, and she started yelling at the Shona woman for not cutting her meats properly. The manager continued to serve our line and told the white woman that he was sorry, but that if she wanted to be served, she'd have to go back in line and wait her turn. She stormed out of the store without the meats. I turned to my friend and said that the words of Paul to the Philippians had just been fulfilled: "Do nothing from selfish ambition or conceit, but in humility regard others as better than yourself. Let each of you look not to your own interests, but to the interests of others" (Phil 2:2–3). Life, indeed, has a sense of humor, for when you always think of yourself as first, you

---

13. Tinker, *Missionary Conquest*, 188–19.

either become last or become disappointed. It is important for everyone to be viewed equally as a child of God. Colonization of the mind is buried so deep in some of the indigenous people's psyche that it is hard for them to believe themselves to be equals to Westerners.

As stated earlier, the two forces of colonialism and Christianity brought with them a mixed bag of changes—both positive and negative. There are examples, however, of missionaries such as bishop Ralph Dodge (more will be presented on him later) in southern central Africa, who fought for African equality and education.[14] One could argue there were positives that came out of the new educational system introduced by colonialism, but even more could have happened had it been instituted with the intent of developing indigenous people. However, in many instances, what the colonizer intended for harm, the indigenous people used to their advantage.

The Subjugation of Knowledge through Education

It is true that in many of the indigenous settings, the native people were introduced to systems of reading and writing, which continue to work to their advantage to this day. They've seen some of the benefits brought about by the new educational system, of being able to read and write, and took advantage of them. On the other hand, the new system also created havoc mentally in the way it was introduced. The intent of the colonizers was to educate the indigenous people for the sake of easy communication and to train them to be servants of the colonizers. Dickson Mungazi cites the educational policy for Africans by the colonial government in 1904 in Rhodesia (Zimbabwe) as saying,

> It is cheap labor that we need in this country, and it has yet to be proven that the Native who can read and write turns out [to be] a good laborer. As far as we can determine, the Native who can read and write will not work on farms and mines. The official policy is to develop the Natives on lines least likely to any risk of clashing with Europeans.[15]

The colonizers' system of education for the natives was not intended for the natives to use, but for their abuse. The colonizer did not see

14. Details about this United Methodist bishop's efforts to fight for equal rights in governance and education for the Africans will be given later in this chapter.

15. Mungazi, *Colonial Education for Africans*, 8.

education as a right for the indigenous people but as a means to acquire economic gain for themselves. Mungazi goes on to say,

> It is clear that the government was not interested in any other form of education for the Africans except for manual labor and practical training. In a fashion that was typical of the attitude of the colonial government, one official explained the reason for this policy as a means of controlling the education of the Africans: I do not consider it right that we should educate the Native in any way that will unfit him for service. The Native is and should always be the hewer of wood and the drawer of water for his white master.[16]

The colonial educational system was unjust; so especially was the intent on which it was established by the colonizers. Doris Lessing shares the view that the education of natives was never intended for their self-development, but for the white colonialists' benefit: "For there was no education in the early days of Southern Rhodesia, except what the Missions provided. The whites believed that an educated 'munt' or 'kaffir' or 'nigger' or 'Jim Fish' was 'spoiled' because 'he got ideas into his head' and always got above himself."[17] The education of indigenous people was only intended for better service to white masters.

One of the goals of narrative counseling or narrative therapy is to work with marginalized communities for justice. Michael White from Australia, one of the founders of narrative therapy (conversations), sees one of the goals of narrative therapy as community work, meaning giving voices to communities whose freedom of expression has been usurped. Jill Freedman and Gene Combs say the following about the work of Michael White and David Epston in starting the narrative-therapy movement:

> He [White] and David Epston, along with others, have developed ways of thinking and working that are based on bringing forth the "discontinuous, particular, and local" stories of individuals and groups, and performing meaning on those stories so that they can be part of an effective "insurrection of subjugated knowledges," an insurrection that lets people inhabit and lay claim to the many possibilities for their lives that lie beyond the pale of the dominant narratives.[18]

16. Ibid., 9.

17. Lessing, Foreword, xv.

18. Freedman and Combs, *Narrative Therapy*, 40.

The need for the resurrection and "insurrection" of the indigenous people's "subjugated" wisdom integrated with the contemporary knowledge is at the heart of this writing. Michael White borrows the idea of "subjugated knowledges" from Michel Foucault. Foucault is a French philosopher who has written much on power, knowledge, deconstruction, and other topics. Foucault says about "subjugated knowledges":

> a whole set of knowledges that have been disqualified as inadequate to their task or insufficiently elaborated: naïve knowledges, located low down on the hierarchy, beneath the required level of cognition or scientificity. I also believe that it is through the re-emergence of these low ranking knowledges, these unqualified even directly disqualified knowledges . . . particular, local, regional knowledge incapable of unanimity, and which owes its forces only to the harshness with which it is opposed by everything surrounding it—that it is through the re-appearance of this knowledge, of these local popular knowledges, these disqualified knowledges, that criticism performs its work.[19]

Colonialism and Christianity subjugated and disqualified the local, religious, indigenous knowledges as unscientific, primitive, and pagan. It is this indigenous wisdom that in this book I argue to reclaim and blend with the knowledge of the contemporary context to forge a better future. Indigenous people, and more specifically those on the African continent, can no longer look totally to the traditional way of life to solve today's problems. Neither can they look to the Western way of life to address their problems in their contemporary context. Most of the people of neocolonial nations today live in between worlds. They feel the pull of the traditional world and the push of the modern world.

Just as Simba's new freedom demanded his taking new path, today's African environment demands that its people find new paradigms in dealing with modern-day crises. Neither the traditional methods alone nor the Western-introduced approaches will suffice. There is need for a blending of new methods in order to serve the modern-day African. A blending of the traditional methods with new Western approaches to form new paradigms is what is needed for today's indigenous contexts. The following section is an attempt to highlight some of the events that

19. Foucault, *Power/Knowledge*, 82.

led to the creation of hybridity in indigenous contexts, resulting in bi-culturalism and bireligiousness.[20]

The Subjugation of Languages

The coming of colonialism created new dominant narrative for the natives. The colonizers forced themselves on the natives and set up a new compulsory system of education, including imposing the content of what was to be learned. Africans had to learn European history, literature, and stories, in addition to new religious doctrines and faith. African history was not taught even though the natives remembered and passed it orally. Shakespeare's writings became the main content of study. English, French, Portuguese, or German became the language of instruction, depending on the colonizer's country of origin. Native languages were not tolerated on school premises, except during designated times; during undesignated times, its use resulted in pupils being shamed and ridiculed.

The colonizers believed that nothing could be learned from the natives wherever they were found. They were considered backward, primitive, and of inferior nature. The many uses of animals in the natives' folktales were equated with how close the indigenous people were to animals mentally and behaviorally. Their stories, myths, symbols, and folktales were to be rid of. Their languages were barbaric and too primitive to be learned. Ngugi wa Thiong'o says this about some of the goals of the colonizers: "The first was to suppress the languages of the captive nations. The culture and the history carried by these languages were thereby thrown onto the rubbish heap and left there to perish. These languages were experienced as incomprehensible noise from the dark Tower of Babel."[21]

The change in language forced by the colonizers on the colonized was intended to change their culture as well. The forced change was not for the purposes of trade or jus a means of communication; it was a way to control the minds of the indigenous people. Ngugi argues further:

> Scandinavians know English. But they do not learn English in order for it to become the means of communication among themselves in their own countries, or for it to become the carrier

20. Mucherera, *Pastoral Care from a Third World Perspective*, 9ff.

21. Thiong'o, *Moving the Centre*, 31.

of their own national cultures, or for it to become the means by which foreign culture is imposed on them. They learn English to help them in their interactions with English tourism, and other links with foreign nations. For them English is only a means of communication with the outside world. . . . English is not a substitute for their languages. . . . Needless to say, the encounter between English and most so-called Third World languages did not occur under conditions of independence and equality. English, French, and Portuguese came to the Third World to announce the arrival of the Bible and the sword. . . . it is the gun which made possible the mining of this gold and which affected the political captivity of their owners. It was language which held captive their cultures, their values, and hence their minds.[22]

Western standards of life and knowledge represented the "truth" that the world needed to know and understand. Colonizers' dispossessing indigenous people's language and power had and still has an impact on the practice of narrative pastoral counseling.

The two elements of language and power are key in the practice of narrative pastoral counseling today. Language both possesses meaning and is power. Language is not a matter of putting words together; neither is it merely or simply an expression of feelings and thoughts: "Language is not only a representation of our thoughts, feelings, and lives; it is part of a multilayered interaction. The words we use influence the way we think and feel about the world, and in turn, the ways we think and feel influence what we speak about. How we speak is an important determinant of how we can be in the world."[23]

Colonizers dispossessed indigenous people by imperially situating themselves in a power position. Wesley S. Ariarajah says about the colonizers and some of the missionaries:

The confidence which the colonizers had in the superiority of their own culture and religion led them in most cases to reject the culture of the people to whom the gospel was brought. Literature on this history abounds, and there is general recognition that the power relations between the colonizers and the colonized were at the heart of the indignity and rejection faced by peoples around the world. Some argue that these power

22. Ibid., 32.
23. Monk, "How Narrative Therapy Works," 34.

relations are still at work today in the way we relate to one another's theology.[24]

The new regimes had power to dictate what was deemed normal
and abnormal in these contexts. Behaviors, worldviews, and values of
indigenous peoples, which were not familiar to Europeans and were
perceived as abnormal by the European standards, were named patho-
logical, madness, illness, and primitive.

The Subjugation of Religiocultural Practices and Self-Governance

The voices and stories of the Africans were silenced and marginalized in
the new educational systems. The European way of life was the standard
of measure. It is common and acceptable knowledge that Christianity
came packaged together with Western culture. Some of the missionaries did not take advantage of what they perceived as the "notoriously
religious" way of life of the indigenous peoples in spreading the gospel.
Others did not see this religiousness as something to be desired; rather
it was to be stamped out, since it was entirely paganistic. Ambrose
Moyo says,

> At the beginning, Christianity was presented and understood
> as synonymous with the Euro-American cultures out of which
> the missionaries to Africa came. Indeed, Ian Smith, the last
> prime minister of Rhodesia, rejected black majority rule be-
> cause it would mean the end of what he called "a Christian civi-
> lization." The Zimbabwean nationalists rejected the perception
> that Christianity and Western culture were inseparably bound
> together, and in defense of their human dignity, they took up
> arms to fight against a system which, contrary to the message
> of Christ as they understood it, created a gospel and culture al-
> liance that justified a social, economic and political system that
> subjugated, dehumanized and impoverished other peoples and
> their cultures.[25]

The coming of colonization and Christianity intended to break the
African's dark past and bring the dawning of European enlightenment.
Civilization and Christianity meant that the African religious culture

24. Ariarajah, *Gospel and Culture*, xii.
25. Ambrose Moyo, *Zimbabwe*, vii.

had to be countered, changed, and the European culture established in these new lands. Godfrey Kapenzi, a Shona writer from Zimbabwe, says about the missionaries:

> Because of his commitment to cultural imperialism, and because of the desire to attach urgency and significance to his work among the "heathens," he often unscrupulously glamorized and romanticized the "inherent inferiority" and ignominious backwardness' of the African, his "slowness" in learning and overwhelming need to "keep the government in civilized hands." The missionary thus anointed the European as the superior custodian of values, morals and ethics and as the sole measurer of culture, civilization and history. Consequently, imperialism and colonialism were made to look like humanitarian responsibilities.[26]

Europeans claimed that it was due to their superior culture, nature, and skin color that Africans were inferior beings. Some of the missionaries came "as sheep in wolf's skin," with imperialism and racism and a belief in their superiority over the Africans. These missionaries came under the guise of expanding the kingdom of heaven, but they were actually expanding earthly kingdoms. For them, Africans were to be converted physically and spiritually into humans. Not only was the religion of the African heathen, pagan, and evil, but even skin color was to be changed to look like that of white people. The African was not human, but needed to be totally transformed to be anything close to human standards.

For the African, the standard of measure to be human was being white (to the extent that Africans used whitening cream [Ambi] to bleach their dark-skinned faces to look white, and a hot iron to straighten their hair to be like Europeans' hair), and this included letting go of their religions and cultures. Dickson Mungazi says that Cecil John Rhodes, who helped the British colonize most of southern Africa, believed in the superiority of Europeans and that they represented the universal man.

> Europeans were synonymous with the universal man. Although emphasis on the study of man formed a philosophy known as humanism, the concept of humanity excluded the African until studies were conducted to determine whether they were actually human. . . . We must unhesitatingly accept the doctrine

26. Kapenzi, *Clash of Cultures*, 2.

that our superiority over the Natives rests on the color of our skin, civilization and heredity. We must appreciate that we have a paramount monopoly of these qualities and that the natives have been denied them by their primitive culture.[27]

A human being, according to some of these early Europeans, was the African who had mastered the European way of life. Thus some of the missionaries and colonialist rejected the traditional religiocultural counseling and healing methods, and as such, the civilization of the Africans altogether. Godfrey Z. Kapenzi says,

Cultural imperialism displaced pure religious evangelicalism. Consequently, the most distinguishing characteristic of missionary operations in Africa was their almost unanimous refusal to incorporate elements of African religions, rituals, music, and ceremonies in any shape or form within the Christian system of religious thought and practice. . . . under the influence of the sense of racial and cultural superiority, and the accompanying arrogance and self-righteousness, the missionary would not give allowances for the existence of a distinct African civilization. . . . Almost everything the African did, said, and thought was considered heathen, sinful and unchristian.[28]

Humans create culture, and in turn culture helps construct an individual's identity. If one's culture is removed, then one is left with a valueless body because of the loss of self. Colonizers knew that if they could rid indigenous people of their culture, they could create a *tabula rasa* and plant their own ideas in the native minds. The way to remove the indigenous culture was by creating a state of self-hate, and a sense of inferiority concerning the indigenous culture, behaviors, and identity. Colonizers forced indigenous people to believe that the only way to survive was to be European. After creating a void in the culture "home" of the indigenous people, the colonizers embarked on a system of reeducating them about the superiority of the new European culture, creating them in their own image. Culture is as water is to fish, without it humanity "dies." I agree with Ngugi on culture:

Culture has rightly been said to be to society what a flower is to a plant. What is important about a flower is not just its beauty. A flower is the carrier of the seeds for new plants, the

27. Mungazi, *Mind of Black Africa*, 27–29.

28. Kapenzi, *Clash of Cultures*, 18.

bearer of the future of that species of plants. . . . Culture carries the values, ethical, moral and aesthetic by which people conceptualize or see themselves and their place in history and the universe. These values are the basis of a society's consciousness and outlook, the whole are of a society's make-up, its identity. A sense of belonging, a sense of identity is part of our psychological survival. Colonialism through racism tried to turn us into societies without heads. Racism, whose highest institutionalized form is apartheid, is not an accident. It is an ideology of control through divide and rule, obscurantism, a weakening of resistance through a weakening of a sense of who we are. Thus, psychological survival is necessary. We need values that do not distort our identity, our conception of our rightful place in history, in the universe of the natural and human order.[29]

The response that the colonizers and some of the missionaries created in these contexts was that of mistrust, especially in the religion that the missionaries were bringing. It is common knowledge that there was a three-tier response to the new religion (Christianity) of the missionaries: rejection, acceptance, and a sense of ambivalence by the Africans. Colonization was forced on the indigenous people with the only option being to fight it.

Today a counselor or therapist who tries to impose Western theories and approaches in indigenous contexts is perceived with suspicion. It is imperative for a narrative pastoral counselor or therapist to understand some of the traditional religiocultural values before engaging in a helping relationship with people from these indigenous contexts. Anywhere around the world where one intends to introduce a different approach or method or teaching, one must take the Apostle Paul's approach at Athens (Acts 17:16–34) of not condemning the people but starting where they are religiously.[30]

The missionaries who took the approach of understanding the people seem to have had better success, and are the ones we must imitate

29. Ngugi wa Thiongo, *Moving the Centre,* 77.

30. When the Apostle Paul introduced Christianity to the Athenians, he first went around the city to understand what type of religion they practiced. He noticed the people were "extremely religious," per their objects of worship. On one of their altars was an inscription, "to the unknown god." Rather than condemning the Athenians for being pagan in their worshipping an "unknown god," Paul used what they already knew to introduce the new religious teaching—God in Christ as the unknown God they were worshipping.

today. The next section addresses the fact that not all missionaries came with the intentions of colonizing everyone. As much as many people in indigenous contexts perceived the missionary endeavors with mixed reactions, due mainly to the oppression brought about by colonization, there were many missionaries who were martyred or deported for fighting oppressive regimes on behalf of indigenous people.

From Subjugation to Hope: The "Remnant-Stump" Missionaries

Sometimes it was hard for indigenous people to distinguish between the good and the bad missionary. A common description of early Christian missionaries is that the distinction between a missionary and a colonizer was that one carried a gun and the other carried a Bible and a gun.[31] This mind-set is even further complicated by the fact that some missionaries not only carried the Bible and a gun, but carried the Bible to conceal their real motives. In addition, a common saying among indigenous peoples that "the cross followed the flag" holds true in many formerly colonized states. Common knowledge about the order of events in the colonization process seems to be as follows: the gun (conquering to enlarge the colonizer's kingdom), gold (the colonizer expanding economically), and God (missionaries spreading the gospel). This order held true everywhere colonization was imposed.

Soon the indigenous people learned, however, that while there was always a "stump that remained," not all missionaries were out to expand their earthly kingdoms. The sole purpose of some missionaries was to preach the gospel of salvation in Jesus Christ. These missionaries believed that indigenous people were created in the image of God. The first Christian missionary martyr in southern central Africa was Father Gonçalo da Silveira. Antonio Fernandes, a Portuguese emissary, preceded Silveira's arrival in the Monomotapa kingdom in 1511. It is said that the Portuguese exploited the discovery of gold among the Monomotapas. It is under these circumstances that Silveira arrived in the kingdom. Silveira had no motives to conquer the kingdom but was focused on preaching the gospel.

---

31. Indigenous people had a hard time distinguishing the missionaries from colonizers; therefore, missionaries were held in suspicion.

At the time of his arrival in Monomatapa, da Silveira was in his middle thirties. . . . The priest reached Mozambique in 1560; that September he set out for the Monomatapa's capital, paddling up the Zambezi in a canoe as far as Tete, and from there walking to the Monomatapa's court. On Christmas Day 1560 da Silveira celebrated the first Christmas mass ever to be recorded in Rhodesia and the next day, the anniversary of St. Stephen the first Christian martyr, the priest walked down the Zambezi escarpment to meet the reigning Monomatapa, Nogoma. Nogoma was an impressionable youth at the time. . . . Before the month was out the Monomatapa, together with his mother and 300 courtiers had accepted baptism at da Silveira's hand. . . . Moslem traders at court, who feared that their position was threatened, persuaded Nogoma that his guest was practising witchcraft, and in March 1561 the young Monomatapa agreed in council that this powerful white sorcerer be put to death. Although warned of his danger Father da Silveira refused to abandon his converts. "I am delighted," he told a Portuguese trader, "to receive so happy an ending from the hand of God." He gave all his possessions away, saving only his cassock, surplice and crucifix, and then waited calmly for the end. Death came to Father da Silveira early on the morning of Sunday, 16 March 1561.[32]

The death of Silveira was instigated not by Africans but instead by Portuguese traders. There were times when the colonizers eliminated each other to take over the land, gold, or the like. It was unfortunate that Father Silveira's mission was cut short, and that his goal to bring the good news to the indigenous people of the Monomotapa kingdom was to be fulfilled by other hands. He was warned about his death but believed that what he was doing was for the purposes of building the kingdom of God. Father Silveira's contact with the people of the Monomotapa kingdom occurred before the coming of the British under Cecil John Rhodes.

Rhodes came to conquer and place Rhodesia under the British rule, and in 1890 Rhodes brought Zimbabwe under British rule. This was followed by a war of resistance from the natives, called the First Chimurenga; the word *chimurenga* means "a freedom fight joined by many." Many from the two native tribes, the Shona and the Ndebele, joined in the war (1896–1897). Ultimately the natives were overpowered,

---

32. "Martyrdom of Fr. Goncalo da Silveira, 1561."

and the country remained a colony of the British. Dickson Mungazi, a Shona historian, says:

> The first two administrators of colonial Zimbabwe [Rhodesia], Leander Starr Jameson (from September 10, 1890 to April, 1896), and Earl Grey (from April 2, 1896 to December 4, 1898), shared the views of their mentor and financier Cecil John Rhodes (1853–1901), who expressed his belief in the first stage of colonizing all of Africa and bringing it under British rule for at least a thousand years. But it was the rest of the colonial officials, from William Milton who served from December 5 1898 to October 31 1914, to Ian Smith who served from April 1 1964 to March 3 1979 . . . who lived and functioned by the Victorian views of the Africans and thereby set the two racial groups on a collision course.[33]

It was the Victorian view that Africans were less human than Europeans, which the Africans continued to resist. This led to the second war of liberation (the Second Chimurenga, 1965–1979). The fight for independence in Zimbabwe involved both the natives and many Europeans who were against the oppression of the Africans.

There were missionaries, such as Bishop Ralph Dodge and Rev. Robert E. Hughes of the United Methodist Church, who in 1964 were deported from Zimbabwe (then Rhodesia) for speaking against the Ian Smith regime for oppressing African people. Dodge wrote against the unjust treatment of Africans by the Europeans. In an article published during the Smith regime, Dodge wrote:

> The church must reject categorically all attitudes and practices of racial superiority or inferiority if it is to make any positive impact upon present-day Africa. This is not just because Africans are going through a revolution in their own society; it is because they are *human beings—full* brothers in Jesus Christ. No human being has the right to relegate another to an inferior position on the basis of nationality, race, or cultural background.[34]

Bishop Dodge posed these challenges to the government not only in his writings but in his sermons and public speeches as well. This was

---

33. Mungazi, *Colonial Policy and Conflict in Zimbabwe,* xx.

34. Dodge, "Why Ian Smith Must Fail," 269–73, italics original. (Bishop Dodge and Rev. Robert E. Hughes were deported from Rhodesia during the Smith regime for speaking against the government.)

counter to what the Smith regime stood for, so he was deported together with Rev. Hughes for standing against the government's imperialistic principles. Even after having been deported, Bishop Dodge kept writing against the Smith regime: "Any society in which the interests of the minority are established and maintained by minority control to the disadvantage of the majority is, from a Christian standard, to be judged as wrong."[35]

Adrian Hastings acknowledges very well the fact that there always had been a "mix up of church and state" where some missionaries, such as Francisco de Montclaro Barretto, were deputy commanders.[36] Hastings, however, further writes about missionaries the likes of Johannes Theodorus Van der Kemp, John Phillip, and John Colenso, who were very unpopular in South Africa among the settlers for preaching equality. In South Africa in the 1950s, Geoffrey Clayton, Ambrose Reeves, and Joost de Blank rose against apartheid.

In then Rhodesia, John White and Arthur Shearly Cripps spoke against oppression of Africans by the colonial government. Bishops Kenneth Skelton and Donald Lamont found themselves forced either to leave the country or to face deportation because of their opposition of the Smith regime. Doris Lessing also wrote against the Smith regime:

> Where is our myopia operating as we read yet another record of stupid brutality—like this one, of British behavior in Rhodesia, from our conquest of the country until now? The white people who speak for Rhodesia and Rhodesians in print, on the air, on television, have spent their entire lives being waited on by black people, who they believe are inferior, whose languages they don't speak, whose culture and history they do not know, whose feelings they have always ignored or insulted.[37]

Wesley S. Ariarajah adds the point that some of the missionaries came specifically to preach the gospel, not to conquer. Some must be given credit for their hard work and their commitment to working for the betterment of the indigenous people.

> In every country to which the missionary message was taken, there are fascinating stories of individual missionaries who

---

35. Ibid., 269–73.

36. Hastings, "Mission, Church and State," 22–32.

37. Lessing, Foreword, xx.

worked selflessly for the betterment of peoples. Some labored tirelessly to preserve local culture by committing ancient stories to writing and translating and making them known to the world. There were also missionaries and converts who tried to work out the meaning of the gospel in a specific culture. Often these attempts to indigenize the gospel took the form of adapting local customs, practices, festivals and dress, but there were also efforts to interpret the gospel within the thought-patterns or theological assumptions of other cultures.[38]

There is no denying that damage was done. However, some of the missionaries came with good intentions, and credit must be given to those missionaries who labored for the sake of the kingdom of heaven. Bishop Eben K. Nhiwatiwa, in his book on the history of the United Methodist Church in Zimbabwe, writes about Bishop Dodge as one who advocated for the education of indigenous people so that they could take over in leadership in the church and even in the government. Nhiwatiwa says, "Rightly so, Bishop Dodge is remembered for the massive program in which numerous young men and women were sent overseas for higher education. . . . [He] was deliberate in his preparation of Africans for leadership positions in the Church."[39]

Bishop Dodge openly wrote advocating for the need for the training of Africans to be administrators in key positions in both the government and the church. He said:

> The major blind spot of the total missionary program in Africa may well be the failure of European church leaders to foresee the approaching rebellion and to train nationals for administrative responsibility. Although some colonial governments have shown interest in educating the masses in central Africa, none have set about training Africans realistically for administrative responsibility under a democracy. There has been a failure to read the signs of the times. Too often, there has been the erroneous idea that economic advancement would satisfy the African people—as if man ever lives by bread alone! Too often, the denominations have followed government for, say, a fifty-year period of gradual turnover. Consequently, there has been

38. Ariarajah, *Gospel and Culture*, 3.

39. Nhiwatiwa, *Humble Beginnings*, 149–50.

no urgency in helping Africans get the necessary training for administrative responsibility.[40]

These few missionary examples could not do as much since they were deported, detained, or sometimes heavily censored by their governments. However, these missionaries' efforts combined with the (natives) majority's resistance were not in vain, as independence from the minority Smith government was ultimately achieved in 1980.

Spiritual Freedom: A Relevant Worship Style

In 1980, Zimbabwe gained independence from the minority and British rule. Many of the missionaries, such as Bishop Dodge of the United Methodist Church mentioned above, also fought for the freedom of African Christian worship. Previously any type of worship that resembled the African traditional style of worship was not acceptable. It was during the 1960s that African drums, shakers, and dance were slowly reintroduced into the Methodist Church. If the gospel of Christ was to take root, it had to be done within the context of the African style of worship. The African Christian story, theology, and worship had to be done from the perspective, worldview, and culture of the people. In many of the mainline churches, changes slowly began taking place. It is, however, a process that is still unfolding even today; many rituals need to be contextualized to fit the African cultural setting.

Later many of the missionaries realized what Bishop Dodges and the others had been saying. The best way to introduce a plant to a new environment is to sow the seed, rather than transplanting the shrub or tree. One who tries to transplant a plant must realize that the plant is already in a culture of certain minerals, and other factors, and may not adapt well in the new culture. The approach of trying to transplant the gospel without being sensitive to the cultures of the indigenous people proved a failure. Even though some never intended the subjugation of natives, there are many natives who struggle today with their spiritual and psychological identity because of the subjugation that took place, and in some cases that has been perpetuated.

Against this history and backdrop, we can begin to understand the situation in Zimbabwe today. The history is that of a people who never

40. Dodge, *Unpopular Missionary,* 22.

lost hope but lived through subjugation, *into* hope. Chapter 3 presents the grim picture of the Zimbabwean situation today. The church, however, has been a beacon of light even during the darkest hours for indigenous people. The church, having taken the lead in the past, can revive hope today and keep that hope alive for tomorrow. Chapter 4 presents "signposts" of hope and reasons why people continue to hold on to hope in the face of poverty and the HIV/AIDS pandemic. It is my conviction that the work of the church in rebuilding community in the name of God is foundational to reviving hope among the widows, the orphans, the HIV/AIDS infected, and the poor. The way of the palaver as presented in chapter 5 can provide that space for these people within the context of the church. Finally, a holistic, narrative pastoral counseling approach is presented using the palaver setting along with illustrative case studies.

In the next chapter, I will introduce from colonialism's earliest days its impact on the community, on family systems, and on the culture of the Shona. I will also give a quick survey of postcolonial (neocolonial) Zimbabwe. Some Africans still carry physical scars form the Second Chimurenga (1965–1979), but it is the many who still struggle with psychological wounds and the pain of cultural dislocation that are of special concern. Also, many today have become cultural refugees because of urbanization. The next chapter will also address the clash of cultures, issues of the coming of the HIV/AIDS pandemic, the borrowed and contrary Western ethical values, such as confidentiality, packaged together and brought to Africa to fight the disease, the stigmatization of the disease, and the politics of it all.

2

Clashing Cultures and Ethical Values in the Age of HIV/AIDS

"Mombe yehumai kama wakaringa nzira."
("One cannot depend on the milk of a borrowed cow
from a mother-in-law.")

—Shona proverb

INDIGENOUS CONTEXTS ARE depending too much on Western-borrowed values, economic ideas, knowledges, cultures, religion, time, technologies, and the like, which are, in the end, destroying their communities. Due to dependency on borrowing, even that which is theirs seems easily taken away from them.

Living by Borrowed Ethical and Cultural Values

It is a well-known fact that most indigenous contexts have been experiencing and will continue to experience cultural changes because of the influence of colonization and modernization. There is no culture that is static; all cultures are dynamic. However, when the change is imposed, and many times too fast, it becomes overwhelming for individuals, communities, or cultures to cope with the rapid social, structural, and systems adjustments. The African context still struggles today with some of the rapid changes that took place due to colonization. The people are caught between worlds and cultural systems: the traditional socioeconomic culture and the modern Western systems. These factors influence ways in which problems are resolved. The traditional systems are alive and well in some parts of rural areas, while in cities many of the people operate from Western systems. In this chapter, I address the issues of cultural conflict, which has created a generation of cultural refugees and a breakdown in the traditional family systems. It is my contention that cultural changes and clashes in ethical values have contributed to the spread of the HIV/AIDS pandemic. In this chapter, you will also be introduced to the politics of the coming of the HIV/AIDS pandemic to contexts such as Zimbabwe.

Even after more than a century of colonization, many in Zimbabwe still maintain two homes, one in the rural areas and another in the city. The idea of having two homes was not the indigenous people's own creation, but was something that was forced on them by the needs of the colonial system. During colonialism, men went into the towns and cities to work. The women stayed in the rural areas and maintained the rural home, farmed the land, and raised the children. This created a change in the family system where men became migrant workers between the cities and the rural homes, and the women maintained the rural home. Michael F. C. Bourdillion, an ethnographer and former professor at the University of Zimbabwe, writes about the changes that took place during early urbanization, some of which are still true today:

> Even while they are still working, many migrants have to utilize their rural property rights. Housing shortages in the towns and cities and, until recently, residential rules for the families of black domestic servants in white owned suburbs, have made it impossible for most workers to have their wives and families with them while they were away from home: these had to remain in their rural homesteads . . . [B]esides the incomes, most men received supplementary sources of food for their wives and growing children, and they obtained this supplementary food by the cultivation of rural holdings, which also provide security against unemployment through redundancy or bad health.[1]

Under these structures, in some rural homes the mother became the disciplinarian and the head of the household while the father was away. Most of the husbands would come home at month's end, and for those who could afford the trip, during the weekends, only to find their family role had changed. These changes in family systems survived into the neocolonial or postcolonial era and into the present.

1. Bourdillon, *Shona Peoples*, 90.

The changes in family structural systems with husbands being migrant workers have contributed to many social problems. Some of the problems this arrangement created are prostitution and *mapoto*—a married man cohabiting with another woman in the city while the wife is in the rural home. Due to long separation periods, some men who found it difficult to maintain fidelity would look for another woman (a mistress) with whom to live in the city. During the initial days of urbanization, single women were mainly found in the rural areas, but those who wanted to make money fast found their way into the cities, depending on prostitution as a way of making a living. Some men took advantage of this, while other men chose *mapoto*. The *mapoto* woman served the man's domestic needs (cooking, washing, etc.), and after he returned home tired from long hours of working, she served his sexual needs. I will address this issue further in chapter 3, since this has significantly contributed to one of the main problems with the spread of HIV/AIDS in this context.

The Zimbabwean people never accepted these arrangements, but some continue to practice them. Bourdillon says about the colonial system and the creation of *mapoto*:

> Although many Shona think of *mapoto* unions as similar to prostitution, and although both are relatively new to Shona society, brought about largely by urban environments, the two are very different. There are a number of factors encouraging prostitution in urban areas. One is the desire of relatively poor women to acquire a certain economic independence from their husbands, which may result in limited clandestine prostitution. Another is the desire of girls to be free of kin and of unpleasant domestic service. Certainly, a girl can, through prostitution, earn an income that allows her to live in a style far beyond the means of most women. Married women usually shun prostitutes . . . and professional prostitutes are usually quite open about the way in which they make their living.[2]

It is through some of these *mapoto* relationships that HIV has infected other men; however, there is more to HIV infection than these *mapoto* relations. Some of the women willing to cohabit may lead a life of prostitution before agreeing to be a mistress, and thus may already be carriers of HIV. In some situations the man will catch the virus in

---

2. Ibid., 321.

the city and then, when returning to the rural home, spread the virus by having sex with his wife.

Those who have chosen to live in the city still must maintain relationships with relatives in the rural areas in case of family crisis where the extended family is needed, such as funerals. On this, Bourdillon says the following:

> The Shona peoples today are not the Shona peoples of pre-colonial times, not even the peoples of thirty years ago. The Shona are involved in a process of change from a culture without literature and with little technology and little centralization, to a culture that incorporates a growing knowledge derived from literature, and dense population centers to meet the growth of the industry. This change leads people in divergent directions, but all are caught up in it and all must adapt to it. Although some may hanker after the simplicity and surety of an idealized past, the Shona past was a response to an environment that, both physically and socially, has been surpassed and can never return.[3]

Some parents have chosen the city to be their home. Their children have been raised in the city and do not know much about the rural lifestyle. These children can easily be at a loss when they visit their relatives in the rural areas. The same can be said of the children who grow up in the rural areas and have never been exposed to city life. It is my argument that the children reared in the rural areas might have an advantage, because even though they might not be physically exposed to city life, they have been exposed to it through school and the media. Yet, these children have the added advantage of being exposed to the traditional way of life.

For those children born and raised in the city, the condition has created a context of what I term *cultural refugees*. This is a generation of children who do not have a particular culture with which they can fully identify. They are neither fully Shona nor Western in their identity and culture. Some parents try to send their children born in the city to the rural areas during the holidays to learn of the traditional cultural practices. But it is not easy for these children, as they find it hard to fit into a place where there is such lack of the conveniences that they usually find in the city, such as electricity and running water in houses. Bourdillon also comments on this:

3. Ibid., 329–30.

"*Chitaundi*" can refer to the culture and customs of the towns as well as to language. The language, which is clearly Shona in structure and style though half the words may be English, typifies the many changes that have taken place as Shona culture adapts itself to town life: new institutions and new ways of life fit themselves into the older social patterns, with which the new town dwellers are familiar and which they adapt appropriately to produce a culture which is neither Western nor traditionally Shona. . . . Many inhabitants of the towns have been born and brought up in an urban environment and many others have spent over half their lives in the towns. It is hard for these to give up the comforts of town life to revert to the more primitive rural life, and few intend to do so if they can possibly avoid it. Some have no real ties with rural relations and would find it impossible to find a rural home even if they wished to. They are town or city people who would find themselves at a loss in the country: town is their home and they have no other.[4]

The parents who have exclusively chosen the city as their home have created a generation of children in Zimbabwe nicknamed *masalala* or *maslads*. This is derived from the word salad. A salad is a mixture of many cut-up vegetables such as tomatoes, lettuce, carrots, etc. The nickname here refers to the fact that the children are exposed to many bits and pieces of the different cultures, both traditional and modern. The little pieces of information these children have about traditional life come from reading books, watching TV, and gleaning from their parents, who also live between cultures every day. In this way, the children are able to embrace neither Shona culture nor Western culture, because all they know are little pieces of these cultures. Hence their lifestyle reflects neither the traditional nor the Western way of life. Much of the Western culture with which they may tend to overidentify is also learned from Western media and books. Even in their speech, they use mixed words of Shona and English, sometimes nicknamed "Shongilish." This generation has a tendency to view most of the traditional culture as primitive and backward.

It is important to understand the historical context and the bigger picture of these contexts for one's help to be relevant. The problem of HIV/AIDS, which is one of the focuses of this book, has to be understood contextually. HIV/AIDS was first discovered 1984: four years after

4. Ibid., 311–12, italics original.

a twelve-year war of independence in Zimbabwe, and while the rapid changes in the social and family systems discussed above were taking place. Understanding this background helps those doing work with the orphans, and especially in the effort of trying to re-create the palaver. The palaver becomes that place where they can talk about the unspeakable—sex, which if not talked about may leave the children to stumble into the much less publicly talked about deadly killer—HIV/AIDS.

Having given a background to the changing culture of the modern Zimbabwe, it is of dire importance that we understand the issues of HIV/AIDS, politics, conflicts in ethical values, human rights versus the health aspects of the disease, and stigmatization; and then later, chapter 3 will address the issues of poverty and HIV/AIDS. All these are areas one needs to pay close attention to before considering the solutions. HIV/AIDS is a multifaceted problem that does not have one particular solution. It is the goal of this book to present the dynamics of the problem of HIV/AIDS and some of the approaches needing consideration in fighting the pandemic, such as the re-creation of the palaver. The following section will address the issues of the politics of HIV/AIDS in the Zimbabwean (African) context.

Politics, Ethical Values, and HIV/AIDS in Africa

The discovery of HIV/AIDS in Africa had many from the Western scientific world reach back to their misguided notions and claims from the past about who indigenous people really were, especially the African. As presented in the previous chapter, the racist attitudes—that Africans were closer to animals than they were to humans—resurfaced. In addition, the racist stereotype of most colonists, which said that Africans could not control their sexuality, was revived and corresponding conclusions were reached as to why there were so many HIV/AIDS infections in Africa. It is a shame that some of the Western scientists today have brought back the theories that Africans are less human and more like animals; according to such theories, therefore, just as animals, Africans cannot control their sexual desires. African scholars Rosalind Harrison-Chirimuuta and Richard Chirimuuta have closely followed these debates and have written extensively on the issue. They have written in response to the origins of HIV/AIDS, and on how racism has plagued the issues of the pandemic. The following is taken from an article they wrote based on one of their books, about how the issues of HIV/AIDS have been clouded by "shoddy" science and ill-conceived views:

> AIDS researchers have claimed that Africans inject themselves with monkey blood or give their children dead monkeys as toys. Africans have rejected these claims as preposterous. Even for the minority of Africans who hunt and eat monkeys, the prospects for human infection with even a mutant strain of SIV would be remote. . . . Within the scientific literature about AIDS and Africa all the racist themes can be found underpinning arguments for which scientific evidence is contradictory or absent:
>
> • Africans are primitive peoples living in isolated tribes cut off from civilization, so they could have harbored diseases for centuries before they spread to the rest of the world.
>
> • They are evolutionarily closer to monkeys, thus could more readily acquire monkey diseases, perhaps by having sexual relations with monkeys or at least involving them in their sexual practices.
>
> • They are sexuality unrestrained, and a sexually transmitted disease would therefore spread more rapidly amongst them than any other people.
>
> • Their intelligence is limited and they cannot understand the complexity of a disease such as AIDS, and their objections to being attributed with its source are harmful to themselves and do not need to be taken seriously.[5]

I agree with Richard and Rosalind Chirimuuta that there will not be much effort to help those who are infected in the indigenous context if those who are doing the research on the virus seem to be prejudiced against the victims of HIV for causing their own predicament.

It has been discovered there are different types or strains of HIV that are infecting people all over the world today. It has also been well documented that the type that is receiving the most attention in research is the one mostly found in the West, and nothing much is being done on the type (which tends to be the most aggressive) found in southern Africa. These are factors in the politics of HIV/AIDS unknown by most people. Helen Jackson writes:

> HIV-2 is mostly found in West Africa and does not spread the same way HIV-1 does. Also HIV-1 has subtypes from A to J.

---

5. Harrison-Chirimuuta, "Is AIDS African?" This article is based on Chirimuuta and Harrison-Chirimuuta, *AIDS, Africa and Racism.*

Subtypes in Africa are A, C, D, F, G, H and J. North America, Europe, Japan and Thailand have subtype B. Much work has been done for researching subtype B and there is more needed research on the other subtypes. HIV 1 C is dominant in Southern Africa and is the most aggressive, spreading faster than the other HIV-1 subtypes.[6]

It is common knowledge that many of the Western pharmaceuticals control the patents on most of the HIV-treatment drugs, and it has been an uphill battle for local companies in developing countries to procure the rights to produce the antiretroviral drugs in generic form for cheaper costs. A medical humanitarian organization, Médecins Sans Frontières (MSF, also known as Doctors Without Borders) said the following about the politics involved in HIV-treatment drugs and universal access to medicine:

> As the World Health Organization (WHO) and UNAIDS release a long-awaited report on their '3x5' AIDS treatment initiative and call for universal access, the medical humanitarian organization Médecins Sans Frontières (MSF) is expressing concern that not enough is being done to make sure that the drugs needed to expand and sustain treatment are accessible to those who need them. . . . At the same time, the World Trade Organization's (WTO) rules on patents are threatening to dry up sources of low-cost generic versions, including some of the first-generation drugs. Without a reliable supply of low-cost AIDS drugs, national governments and treatment providers will be faced with an uphill battle, and patients risk having vital treatment interrupted or priced out of their reach . . . Pharmaceutical companies are faster in filing patents in developing countries than in delivering the drugs.
>
> As an example, Abbott Laboratories only sells in the US a new version of the World Health Organization recommended second-line AIDS drug (lopinavir/ritonavir) that is particularly suited for use in developing countries because it does not need refrigeration. MSF placed an order for the drug with the company's headquarters in Chicago but, so far, Abbott has refused to proceed with filling the order and there are no alternative sources for this product today. MSF warns that, if there is no concerted effort by the UN and the international community to

6. Jackson, *AIDS Africa*, 84.

make sure there is a steady supply of low-cost AIDS drugs, attaining the goal of universal access will remain impossible.[7]

It is all about money and control, not about saving those who are dying of the disease. Western companies that have more power and control of the market prevent even a country such as South Africa, which has the means to produce the drug in generic form, from saving its own people.

Our economies are headed by unrepentant, greedy leaders who only think of themselves and not about the poor in their countries. At the international level, we have the World Bank, and the International Monetary Fund, which do not seem to care about the well-being of the poor in poor countries; instead, their goals are profit making. They make the poor countries suffer by imposing impossibly heavy interest rates on them. The humanitarian agencies Oxfam and ActionAid blame the world's richest countries for the poverty in developing countries:

> Only one-fifth of global aid is actually going to the world's poorest countries, say humanitarian agencies. Oxfam and ActionAid, in a joint report, accuse the wealthiest nations of failing the poor with a "self-serving and hypocritical" system of aid. They say up to 40% of aid is 'tied', forcing developing countries to buy overpriced goods from donor countries. The report calls for reforms, as international development ministers meet in Paris to discuss global aid. "Our report tells a sorry tale of muddle and hypocrisy, dithering and stalling, with the world's poor cast unwittingly in the role of the fall guys," says Patrick Watt, ActionAid's policy officer. But the report claims that wealthy nations are failing to deliver on their pledges. It says just one-fifth of aid actually goes to the poorest countries— and only a half of that is spent on basic services such as health and education. The agencies accuse rich countries of "using aid to reward strategic allies and pet projects at the expense of the neediest countries."[8]

The economic system of capitalism was introduced by colonialism. Neocolonial governments inherited this system and have continued it. These systems, perpetuated by neocolonial governments in most

---

7. Médecins Sans Frontières, "As WHO and UNAIDS Call for Global Treatment Scale-Up."

8. BBC, "Global Aid Failing Poor Nations."

indigenous contexts, are based on the Western economic standards that stand in contrast to traditional ways. The traditional indigenous economies operated on the basis of the principle: "as you take care of your own needs, keep in mind those of your neighbor who does not have enough." Similar to biblical times (Lev 19:9–10, Deut 24:19–21, Ruth 2:1–9⁹), Africa's traditional prosperous farmers, especially in Zimbabwe, never harvested all the grain out of their fields for the sake of the poor. The capitalistic Western economic system has since put them in conditions where they live by the rules of the jungle: survival of the fittest; each person for him- or herself and God for us all. The idea of the village has been lost. The gap between the poor and the rich has widened. Those in power do not seem to care much about the welfare of the poor since they (the rich) have enough at their tables—they never go hungry. The rich are reaping everything off their fields, and they even go after whatever little the poor might have. We are back in the days of unrepentant King David and Uriah in the Bible. David lusted after a poor man's (Uriah's) wife, Bathsheba, and then had Uriah killed so he could have her as his own (2 Sam 11:1—12:12). The rich countries are going after the little that the poor countries have and are then leaving them poorer.

There is more going on in our world today than eyes can see and the media portray. Below is another example of how the rich, or the "haves," can tell the "have-nots" what they want, not what they need to survive:

> Forget about rampant inflation, high unemployment, or the fact that more than one million people need food aid. Forget that you are lucky to live beyond thirty-four. Zimbabweans just love sex. That is the impression one gets when one looks at the amount of money being poured into HIV/AIDS when an estimated 1.4 million are said to have no food. The major food donor, the World Food Programme, last month said it might cut down on the number of people it was feeding because it did not have enough food for an estimated 1.4 million hungry people until the end of March next year when the current season's harvest is expected to start rolling in. It said that it would require US$16 million to purchase 26,000 tons of grain needed to meet the anticipated shortfall. At about the same time, Britain said it

---

9. All these passages talk about the laws of harvest in order for the rich to take care of the poor in their communities.

had awarded 20 million pounds (US$38.7 million) to Zimbabwe to fight the HIV and AIDS epidemic. The disease currently affects 1.8 million people. The money would be used to distribute more than 250 million condoms through 700 hair salons over the next five years. International Development Secretary Hilary Benn was quoted as saying: "People should not die because they have sex."

As if to support the appropriateness of the donation, The Sunday Mail reported that Zimbabwe led the world in the use of condoms. Some 163 million male condoms and 3.8 million female condoms—the highest in the world—had been sold in Zimbabwe over the past five years. While the HIV/AIDS epidemic has devastated the country, Zimbabwe is now reportedly winning the war against HIV/AIDS. Prevalence is reported to have declined to 18.1 percent from over 30 percent at one stage. But some 3,200 people are still reportedly dying each week, a figure controversial Roman Catholic Archbishop Pius Ncube says is higher than the deaths in Sudan's war-torn Darfur region. This has prompted some AIDS activists to question why so many people are still dying while the prevalence rate is reportedly declining. Others are questioning the efficacy of aid, who this aid actually benefits, and who determines who needs what?[10]

The above are facts that those who are serious about working with the HIV/AIDS infected and affected must not ignore. These systems must be challenged, and local communities must be given the voice about what is a priority in terms of needs, instead of simply being "grateful" for whatever one receives. As the old adage goes, "A beggar is not a chooser." Since indigenous communities are the beggars, it follows that they have no choice about what is sent to them. This point will be addressed further in chapter 3, in connection to the issues of HIV/AIDS and poverty.

It is interesting that when studies and research are done, and they contradict the popularly held claims, the research results do not find their way into the main media broadcasts. As much as no one disputes the fact that one of the HIV ports of entry into the body system is through sexual intercourse, there have also been studies showing that in Zimbabwe cases of sexually transmitted diseases increased while new infections of HIV, which can be considered an STD, decreased. The

10. Rukuni, "Forget about Hunger, Zimbabweans Just Love Sex."

following are findings and observations by Gisselquist, an economic anthropologist, in his travels in Central African countries:

> Every major campaign against AIDS in Africa has been based on the premise that heterosexual sex accounts for 90 percent of transmission in adults. Economic anthropologist David Gisselquist therefore suspected that HIV might be spreading primarily by another route. After analyzing 20 years of epidemiological studies, he and his colleagues concluded that unsafe injections, blood transfusions, and other medical procedures may account for most AIDS transmission in African adults. Their analysis indicated that no more than 35 percent of HIV in that population is spread through sex. Gisselquist's interest in AIDS was stimulated by the guidance he received while traveling through Africa as a World Bank consultant. "They give you a syringe and say, 'Carry this with you, and avoid all the health care you can.' We've been praying for third-world health care while advising ourselves to avoid it," he says. When he examined hundreds of papers on AIDS in Africa, he found evidence to back up those concerns. A study in the Democratic Republic of the Congo, for instance, found that 39 percent of HIV-positive, vaccinated infants had uninfected mothers. In contrast, Gisselquist could not uncover any clear data proving that sexual intercourse dominates the spread of African AIDS. In Zimbabwe, HIV incidence rose by 12 percent per year during the 1990s, even as sexually transmitted diseases sank by 25 percent overall and condom use rose among high-risk groups. Gisselquist recently reported his findings in four papers published in the *International Journal of STD & AIDS*.[11]

HIV infection in indigenous contexts such as Zimbabwe cannot be blamed solely on sexual immorality. However, many still generally hold on to the conclusions that those who are HIV infected got it through sexual intercourse. There is no doubt whatsoever that much infection is caused by sexual intercourse, but it is also critical that the issues raised above, which are perpetuating the delay in winning the war against HIV/AIDS, must be addressed. Below is the history of the discovery of HIV/AIDS in Zimbabwe, and my perceived notions on what I see as a collision of ethical values.

---

11. Glausiusz, "Why Do So Many Africans Get AIDS?"

The Discovery and Naming of HIV/AIDS

In Zimbabwe, some of the first cases of HIV are said to have been discovered in 1984. One wonders where the virus had been hibernating in
the years before the discovery. I agree with Musa W. Dube that when
the virus was discovered, many of the people in the indigenous contexts, including Zimbabwe, used to think of it as a "radio disease" or
"city disease," since those who were announcing it were in the city or on
the radio. The disease was named by the Western scientific world. How
could people be afraid of a disease they had never seen someone die
from? The names HIV and AIDS did not translate into any of the local
languages; neither did the maladies themselves resemble any diseases
common in these contexts.[12] The idea of the subjugation of languages
and its impact on people's knowledges was at play in this case, since the
disease was being named "for them."

When people have the knowledge and power to name something,
they have the power and some control over the thing. It is through experience that people can claim knowledge about something; otherwise,
all is information, which in some cases is not useful. It was only when
the people started to name the disease they began to take it seriously.
The old adage that "experience is knowledge, all else is information,"
holds true in this case.

In Zimbabwe today, HIV/AIDS illnesses have been given different
names. It was only after years of Zimbabweans' seeing people and relatives dying without having adequate knowledge about the dynamics of
the pandemic that names translated into the people's experiences were
created. Today in Zimbabwe HIV/AIDS is known by different names,
such as *shuramatongo* or *chivharamagonhi* ("that which closes all village
doors or leaves villages in ruins"), *mukondombera* ("plague"), *tsotsi* or
mbavha ("thief" or "robber"), *chirwere* ("the illness"), *chirwere chemu-
tambo* ("the illness of pleasure"), *gukurahundi* ("early spring rains that
'clean up' after threshing") *chiro* ("an ugly thing"), and *chipuka* ("a scary
animal").

Language and naming has power. In narrative counseling when
one names something, it gives power to the one who names, power
to be able to talk about the "thing" they have named, especially if it
is something that is destroying the community. People can now talk

12. Dube, "Andinkra!" 134–35.

about the pandemic using common language available to them based on experience, not a scientific, laboratory-coined name. These names can be used at the palaver to help people talk about their experiences and their hurt and pain.

The Stigmatization of HIV/AIDS

Stigmatization and the use of confidentiality in working with the HIV/AIDS infected came to most African communities as one package, resulting in patients' choosing to live secretively with the illness. In other words, this was not a disease one wanted to die from; nor did patients wish to tell their families or the community. Thus, for those who found out they were positive, the doctors blessed and covered the information with the borrowed Western blanket of confidentiality. In some of the first burials of HIV/AIDS victims by African pastors, around 1985/1986 in Zimbabwe, bodies came from the hospital in tied black plastic bags, and the people were advised never to open them. There are cases in those early days where some families, still today, do not know whether they buried the right deceased family member. No last body viewing was allowed since people were not sure how the disease was transmitted. Death caused by HIV was not talked about. Preachers castigated those who died of the illness saying the disease was a "disease of pleasure" and directly associated with prostitution. In this case, many preachers' preconceived notions were that those who died from the disease had brought it on themselves. In Papua New Guinea, some AIDS victims are being buried alive by relatives who fear becoming infected themselves: "One was calling out 'Mama, Mama' as the soil was shoveled over his head," said Marabe, who works for a volunteer organization, "If we let them live, stay in the same house, eat together and use or share utensils, we will contract the disease and we too might die."[13]

A Conflict in Values: Secrets versus Confidentiality

There is need to reevaluate some of the systems that have been accepted from the West, and to create ones that will work for the African context in the war against HIV/AIDS. The continent needs to continue to cleanse itself of the "colonial demons" of accepting most of that

13. Agence France Presse, "AIDS Victims 'Buried Alive' in PNG."

which is Western as modern and better.[14] In other words, communities should be permitted to create solutions with those who have financial means to fund these solutions with no strings attached. At the same time, however, many African communities need to reassess some of the traditional practices that appear to foster the spread of the devastating HIV/AIDS disease.

I argue in this section that there is need for African communities 1) to reassess some of the borrowed Western ethical values and practices being enforced today (such as confidentiality), especially in the mental and medical health systems; and 2) to reappraise some of the African traditional values and practices in the face of HIV/AIDS pandemic.

A Reassessment of Some of the Borrowed Western Ethical Values

The HIV/AIDS pandemic, the "new disease," came to the African community enveloped with the ethics of confidentiality. The Western scientific mental and medical health systems dictated how this new disease was to be handled. Most of the local doctors practicing in these contexts were trained using Western methods and guidelines. It was easy, then, for them to accept the guidelines of confidentiality. The local governments did not challenge this requirement, since it was coming from a Western scientific knowledge base.

Confidentiality is one of the main ethical values enforced in the mental and medical health systems, a value that I believe contributed to the spread of the HIV/AIDS pandemic. Confidentiality means an explicit promise to protect a client or patient's information, except under conditions agreed upon by the client or patient, or when there is indication that the client intends to harm self or another.[15] In general, the purpose of confidentiality is usually to protect the patient or client from harm, be it physical, emotional, or spiritual.

On two different occasions, I took a brother-in-law and a close friend who were suspected to be HIV positive to the doctor for tests and the results. When I asked if I could be present for support, I was respectfully told by the workers and the doctors that I could not be present in the room due to confidentiality, and I was told to stay in the

14. Thiongo, *Decolonising the Mind*; Memmi, *Colonizer and the Colonized*; and Nandi, *Intimate Enemy.*

15. James and Guilliland, *Crisis Intervention Strategies,* 82.

waiting area. I thought this was the time my brother-in-law and my friend needed me the most, but based on confidentiality I could not be present in the room when they were being given the results.

At one training session in 2003 when we were offering workshops for pastors and lay leaders of the church on HIV/AIDS in Zimbabwe, we had a community-health worker come to make a presentation. She encouraged people to be tested in order to know their status. In addition, she told those present that doctors and community-health workers, especially those working with HIV/AIDS patients, operate under strict guidelines of confidentiality, and that one's status was between the patient and the doctor. She read to those present the guidelines, which were almost word for word as stated below:

> The rule states that the counselor has an obligation to disclose if, and only if, there is medical evidence that the person is HIV-positive, the person is in a high-risk relationship, there is little likelihood of disclosure by the client. . . . The therapist still has to consider other core issues as well [including] 1) the client's autonomy to choose whom to and when to tell, 2) the counselor's doing no harm to the client, 3) the counselor's doing what is beneficial for the client, and 4) the counselor's being just to the client. Breaching confidentiality would undoubtedly do much harm to all those ethical principles and destroy the relationship between the worker and the client.[16]

Based on these guidelines, once a client or patient tells the counselor or the medical practitioner that they will disclose their HIV status to their spouse or partner, or promises to use protection during sex, the worker cannot disclose their HIV status to another. They must trust the word of the client. The real question is where the ethical consideration for "community human rights" is. All the statements above are about the protection of the individual, but what about the community at large? What ethics is there to protect the community human rights from the individual who could infect others, and also to address issues of public health? Furthermore, the above statements are contrary to the traditional African way of life.

16. Ibid., 85.

Confidentiality: The Secret Weapon of Mass Destruction (WMD)

In most African communities, traditionally, an individual who is infected by a deadly disease must not suffer alone. The adoption of the
Western standards of ethical practices such as confidentiality in addressing the issues of HIV/AIDS is a borrowed value that needs to be
reevaluated for the African community. Confidentiality in mental-
health and medical practice says that the information about the patient's
health is between the patient and the counselor/doctor, except under
the patient's consent. The ethical guidelines say that it is only when the
client is engaging in "high-risk" behaviors and the victim(s) are known,
and when the one infected says they will not tell their spouse or partner, that the worker may disclose information to curtail the behavior
of the HIV-positive person. This ethical practice places more value in
individual human rights, and yet the result is the destruction of life in
community. It is interesting to note that most of those infected die with
their individual rights, but are sadly dying lonely deaths in trying to
keep their HIV/AIDS status a secret. Therefore, confidentiality, in light
of the HIV/AIDS pandemic, has become "a secret weapon of mass destruction" in many African communities.

Dr. Paul Chimedza, a medical practitioner in Zimbabwe, raised
this concern in a column in a local state-run newspaper. I find it worth-
while to quote most of Dr. Chimedza's article here as an example of the
magnitude of the HIV/AIDS problem and the issue of confidentiality.
He writes:

> Sometime in 1999, I was looking after a certain couple living
> positively with HIV and AIDS. The wife then passed away.
> Six months down the line the husband (50 years old) brought
> a 17-year-old girl to me and introduced her as his new wife.
> Naturally, I was very worried that the 17-year-old was going to
> be infected so I secretly raised my concern with the patient and
> implored on him to inform his new wife about his HIV status.
> He said, *Chiremba don't worry, I will strictly and consistently use
> condoms with her and inini ndakura munyaya dzebode, ndava
> kungoda kuti agozondichengetawo. I am not crazy about sex
> anymore. I am just looking for someone to take care of me.* He
> promised to tell her about his status but he never got around to
> doing it. On putting more pressure on him to disclose his status
> to the wife, he changed doctors. Eight months down the line, he
> came back because his wife was now pregnant and he wanted

me to institute measures to prevent infection of the baby by the HIV virus. On doing the HIV test the wife was also now positive. I felt terrible that she had been infected while I looked on. Medical ethics and confidentiality prevented me from informing the young girl that her husband was living positively with HIV and AIDS. She never got the opportunity to take adequate precautions to prevent infection from her husband because she didn't know.

I then thought seriously about the double standards that are occurring with regards to HIV and AIDS compared to other killer diseases. (italics original)

Chimedza goes further to talk about how governments responded to the outbreak of SARS and Ebola. People suspected of being infected by these diseases were easily quarantined and tested. Chimedza continues, asking,

where was the medical ethics and confidentiality? These were rightfully thrown out the window because they were not expedient at that time. These drastic, determined, and decisive measures were necessary, that's why these highly infectious and dangerous diseases were contained. Imagine what would have happened had we treated these two devastating diseases the way we treat HIV and AIDS that is with whispers, exaggerated medical confidentiality, excessive observation of human rights and secretiveness. Our righteous, politically correct selves would have been wiped out of the face of this earth. The same leadership, zeal, decisiveness and determined action just don't seem to happen with HIV and AIDS. We seem paralyzed. There is a certain amount of inertia. We are treating HIV and AIDS not only with kid gloves but also like royalty. We speak about it in whispers and hushed tones like it's too sacred to mention. We won't test it like we did with SARS and Ebola. We frighten people about the possible severity of HIV and then expect these same frightened people to come forward voluntarily and be tested. This just doesn't happen.

Chimedza goes on to say that if a person is diagnosed with tuberculosis (TB) today, those whom he or she has met will be screened for TB with or without permission. If a person is a pilot and has poorly controlled epilepsy, doctors are allowed by law to disclose the condition to an employer. The person is not allowed to fly a plane and put the lives of passengers in danger.

He further asks,

> Again what happens to medical confidentiality here? It is ig-
> nored because in this instance, it will not serve any good pur-
> pose to anyone. No one mentions confidentiality and rights in
> this instance because lots of lives are at stake. Why is it that
> with HIV and AIDS we get so passionate about confidentiality
> and human rights that we watch people getting infected and do
> nothing about it? What about the rights of those being infected?
> I am sure 80% of Zimbabweans who are negative have a right to
> be protected from infection and the 20% who are positive also
> have a right to be protected from re-infection.[17]

Chimedza is right on the mark concerning some of the problems
indigenous contexts face in adopting Western standards, and concerning those standards' being imposed in these settings. As I argued earlier,
we still have situations where, for example, in order for poor countries
to receive donor funds, they have to abide by certain conditions stated
by the donor agency. It is my contention that NGOs (nongovernmental
organizations) or those wanting to help developing countries must do
so without imposing their own standard on the receiving country. The
donor agencies must act as partners in providing the funds, but at the
same time must let the receiving party be self-determining in how best
to utilize the received funding. There must be ways to work with the
local people without imposing the donor's values on those receiving
the help.

HIV/AIDS came with a prescription from Western medicine and
mental-health systems on what doctors and counselors in the indigenous context had to practice if they were to get funding. Within traditional African societal values, one disclosed one's illness to the family or
community for support. The family or community helped find a cure,
and those dying from an illness never neither died alone nor kept their
illness a secret. Confidentiality and the stigmatization attached to HIV/
AIDS created an environment where people experienced, and are still
experiencing, lonely deaths.

One of the worst things that can happen to an African is to be cut
off from one's family or community for any reason. It is a shame that
many of those infected, because they want to keep their status confi-
dential, are experiencing two deaths—relational and emotional—even

17. Chimedza, "Let's Do SARS Act on HIV."

before their physical death. In most African communities, even the witch, the perceived enemy of the community, never died alone. The perimeters of confidentiality in mental and medical health practice are based on Western individual rights and are working counter in the fight against HIV/AIDS. Confidentiality must not kill but instead must preserve life. The most honorable thing the one who is infected could do is to disclose the illness. Why would one knowingly put poison in "a well from which every member of the family or community drinks"? A Shona saying goes: "It is only the witch who refused for people to multiply," by poisoning others through witchcraft. Instead of feeling free to talk about the disease and to live their last days in community, many have become prisoners to confidentiality, doing whatever is necessary to keep HIV/AIDS a secret.

Sex Education and Individual Rights to Privacy

In traditional African communities, sex education was the job of aunts, uncles, elders in the community, and grandparents. Initiation ceremonies marked the boys' and girls' transition from adolescence to adulthood. Due to subjugation and suppression of the traditional cultural practices by Westernization and urbanization, these traditional practices were deemed backward and were actually ended in the cities. However, they still exist in some parts of the communal areas. Michael Gelfand writes about how the aunts and grandparents were traditionally important in the education of girls. He says the following about how girls were expected to participate in the practice called *mucheso* or *kundoonekwa* to keep their virginity until they were married:

> Each adolescent girl (*mhandara*) has to undergo a routine inspection for virginity (*utsvene*). She is taken to the river with other girls of her own age by her grandmother or another elderly woman. They take a small calabash (*kadende*) and a little girl of about three or four years of age. This takes place once a month in some places and in others twice a year until the girl marries. Any elderly woman may perform this examination (*kundoonekwa*). The party leaves early in the morning, the girls all bathe together and then each in turn lies down on the riverbank and is examined by the old woman, who compares their genitalia with that of the little girl. This practice is still performed amongst the *VaBudjga*. They are given babies to suckle. If the girl is pure, she

allows it to such but if not she refuses because she is afraid the baby will develop severe diarrhea if she has misbehaved.[18]

Many children today, especially in the cities, lack the accountability that used to be offered by the aunts or elderly women, in keeping the girls pure until they marry. Experimentation, poor peer education, and the media filled with Western culture have become the sources for children's sex education. It is through experimentation that some of these children may be exposed to the HIV infection.

Aunts and grandparents are at a loss today to communicate with this generation, which tends to mix Shona and English in their everyday conversations. It is frowned upon for children to speak in English to their grandparents. This indicates disrespect of the elder as well as of the traditional culture itself. Usually, speaking in English to elders (especially ones who do not know English) was an indication that the child viewed the elder as ignorant, unlearned, and backward.

There has been a rise in men who are HIV/AIDS positive who are misinformed, who believe that having sex with a virgin will cure AIDS. This is putting many of our little girls, especially orphans, in danger. The British Broadcasting Corporation (BBC) on its Internet site reported the following about the Girl Child Network of Zimbabwe:

> Zimbabwe's most prominent organisation fighting child sexual abuse is confronting traditional healers to take action over the myth that having sex with a virgin can cure Aids—one reason behind the rape of young girls. In a rural area some 200km east of Harare, a play is being acted out. An HIV-positive man visits a traditional healer and is advised to have sex with a virgin in order to be cured. The reasoning is that the blood produced by raping a virgin will cleanse the virus from the infected person's blood. It is part of the Girl Child Network project and was staged at a girl's empowerment village, where rape survivors are given safe accommodation, counseling and training in life–skills. Traditional healers from all of the country's provinces recently attended a meeting here, along with chiefs, a government minister and religious leaders, where many of the girls stood up and gave accounts of the abuse that they had suffered.[19]

---

18. Gelfand, *Growing Up in Shona Society*, 19.

19. Vickers, "Staging Sex Myths to Save Zimbabwe's Girls."

Mucheso is one of those traditional practices that could easily be used today to protect little girls from abusers. Usually those who abuse children tend to threaten them if they tell. Why do we have to wait for the child to be abused before we can offer protection? It has been found that where inspections are done, there is less prevalence of rape or abuse because the men who abuse are afraid of being found out. Isabel Phiri did research in 2002 on virginity testing and wrote a paper based on the interviews she had with Nomagugu Patience Ngobese, a woman leading the revival of traditional virginity testing in Kwazulu Natal Province. Nomagugu says that virginity testing is protecting girls, and it is empowering girls "to say no to sex." In the paper, Phiri says that it appears those who are vehemently opposed to virginity testing base their opposition on a Western worldview:

> For Nokuzola and Nomagugu, they see injustice as not with the ritual of virginity testing, but in HIV/AIDS, teenage pregnancy, and rape of girls and women. . . . Most criticism for the virginity testing is coming with a Western worldview. For Nomagugu and the rest of the mothers and grandmothers who support the ritual, it is about economical and social survival. If the girls do not become pregnant, the grandmothers will not become burdened with looking after the grandchildren. . . . The girls are empowered to say no to sex.[20]

The goal of virginity testing is primarily prevention. Virginity testing is one of those desperate measures—when everyone is desperately looking for a solution to the HIV/AIDS pandemic—that needs examination. In addition, virginity testing helps with early intervention for girls if abuse is found to have occurred. The idea is not to just inspect but to educate the girls as well about their safety, and to hold them accountable. The argument that has been put forth by those who oppose virginity testing is that it is a backward practice and that it invades the little girls' individual rights to privacy. The BBC reported that the deputy president of South Africa (SA), Jacob Zuma, had encouraged virginity testing, but this was easily countered by human-rights groups:

> South African's deputy president has encouraged young girls to take virginity tests to curb the spread of HIV/Aids and teenage pregnancy. Jacob Zuma said it was an African custom for a woman to value her virginity. Early pregnancy leads to children

20. Phiri, "Virginity Testing?"

being abandoned, he said. But human rights groups say the practice of virginity testing is a human rights violation. More than five million South Africans are HIV positive—one in nine people. Virginity testing is practiced in KwaZulu Natal and neighboring Swaziland, where girls lie down on mats for a woman to check to see if their hymens are intact. Mr. Zuma lamented the erosion of traditional African family values, Sapa news agency reports. "Girls knew that their virginity was their family's treasure," Mr. Zuma said speaking at an event near Umtata in the Eastern Cape on Wednesday, where some 40 girls took part in a virginity-testing programme. "They would only have sex when permitted to do so by their families after marriage," he said."[21]

The Western-educated human-/individual-rights groups are the ones who responded negatively to the practice, saying it is traditionally backward, unhygienic, and a violation of individual rights of privacy. This practice is not something new to the African context; it disappeared in the cities due to Westernization but is still being practiced sparingly in some the rural communities. To the Western mind, it is a foreign idea and one that violates one's individual rights, even though in the Western world has gynecologists.

The call for virginity testing is also being made by some of the elders in Murewa.

Elders in Murewa have called for the reintroduction of virginity testing amongst young girls as a means of discouraging them from early sexual engagement that could result in HIV infection. Expressing their concerns at a discussion forum entitled "Addressing HIV/AIDS and Gender Based Violence from a cultural perspective" in Murewa recently, the elders said most girls were engaging in prostitution and this is a major concern if the community is to win the battle against HIV and Aids. Forced virginity testing is a crime under the new Domestic Violence Act. The Southern Africa HIV/AIDS Information Dissemination Service (SAfAids) in partnership with Rozaria Memorial Trust co-hosted the discussion forum that was attended by chiefs, headman and village heads. The elders said they were worried that most girls were prostituting with haulage truck drivers waiting for maize deliveries at the Grain Marketing Board silos.

21. BBC, "SA Leader Urges Virginity Tests."

"Our children are selling wild fruits in the afternoons and their bodies to haulage truck drivers at night. By the time they get married some of them would have been infected by Aids," said a woman who identified herself as Mai Chigwida.

Mrs Chingandu said the aim of the discussion forum is to provide the community with a platform to dialogue and share ideas on how culture can be harnessed to respond to HIV and Aids and gender based violence. The Minister of Health and Child Welfare, Dr David Parirenyatwa who was the guest of honor said there is need to get the right direction on whether to test for virginity or not since some activists argue that it is a violation of human rights to test for virginity.[22]

The response given by the minister of health and child welfare is not surprising, since the current laws of Zimbabwe on this issue are not based on traditional practices; rather they are based on Western standards, which place the practice under human rights and not as a public health issue. Yet, in thinking that we are defending our young defenseless children's individual rights to privacy, we are actually giving them a death sentence and an individual right to their grave by withholding protection, guidance, counsel, and care. What is more important—giving privacy or protecting defenseless children from abuse and encouraging them to share who the perpetrator is if they are found to have lost their virginity? Instead, let us give our children *individual rights to life* by using some of these traditional approaches of protection. The pressing issue is about giving accountability, guidance, and values of self-care to our young girls. I don't believe that parents could openly rejoice at the death of their teenage girl for having afforded her "individual rights to privacy," nor would a teenage girl dying of HIV/AIDS be joyous for having achieved her "individual right to privacy" on her deathbed.

Trained women community-health workers or counselors, as well as church mothers, could undertake this practice as a way to protect these children from abuse or further abuse. If the infection is found early enough, there is time for treatment. And rather than waiting until late in the course of their illness when they're already sick or have signs and symptoms of an HIV-related condition, patients can be treated immediately. How ironic that some African groups are rejecting available

22. "Murewa Elders Call for Virginity Testing."

means at their disposal in favor of the Western approaches (not easily accessible).

Further, as I argued earlier, there is much conflict in ethical values about the issue of HIV/AIDS based on the case by Chimedza. The HIV/AIDS pandemic is more that a human-rights issue; it is a public-health issue. From the time of its discovery in the West, it was made a human-rights problem rather than a public-health problem. The indigenous contexts inherited the placement of the pandemic under human rights rather than public health, and it has been kept that way, even today. The West, especially the USA, is now changing gears on how to face the problem as a public health issue, even though the pandemic has not officially been placed under the category of public health problems.

The West and a New Proposal on HIV/AIDS Testing

The United States Department of Health and Human Services along with the Center for Disease Control (CDC) have proposed mandatory HIV testing for all teenagers and adults between the ages of thirteen and sixty-four. One wonders why the USA has now found it to mandatory to test their people, but the African people are refusing the tried and tested traditional means of virginity testing. As much as the proposal by the CDC does not directly mention this move as a "public health" concern, the measures being proposed are clearly based on public health, not human rights concerns. The following is the CDC proposal:

> All Americans between the ages of 13 and 64 should be routinely tested for HIV to help catch infections earlier and to stop the spread of the deadly virus, federal health recommendations announced Thursday. The U.S. Centers for Disease Control and Prevention said HIV testing should become about as common as a cholesterol check. Nearly half of new HIV infections are discovered when doctors are trying to diagnose a sick patient who has come for care, CDC officials said.
>
> "We know that many HIV infected people seek health care and they don't get tested. And many people are not diagnosed until late in the course of their illness, when they're already sick with HIV-related conditions," said Dr. Timothy Mastro, acting director of the CDC's division of HIV/AIDS prevention. "By identifying people earlier through a screening program, we'll allow them to access life-extending therapy, and also through prevention services, learn how to avoid transmitting HIV

infection to others," he said. Some HIV patient advocates and health policy experts hailed the announcement. They said the guidelines could help end the stigma of HIV testing and lead to needed care for an estimated 250,000 Americans who don't yet know they have the disease. . . . Under the new guidelines, patients would be tested for HIV as part of a standard battery of tests they receive when they go for urgent or emergency care, or even during a routine physical. Patients wouldn't get tested every year: Repeated, annual testing would only be recommended only for those at high-risk. There would be no consent form specifically for the HIV test; it would be covered in a clinic or hospital's standard care consent form. . . . CDC officials have been working on revised recommendations for about three years, and sought input from more than 100 organizations, including doctors' associations and HIV patient advocacy groups. The CDC presented planned revisions at a scientific conference in February. Since then, the CDC has strengthened language on informed consent to make sure that no one is tested without their knowledge, and emphasized the need for doctors to provide information on HIV tests and the meaning of positive and negative results.[23]

Why do we, in the African context, scorn the traditional practices that have been used for ages and are proven to work, yet the Western countries are going to similar measures or mandatory testing that suit their contexts? Is the practice being deemed backwards and unhygienic simply because it is being done by African women who do not meet Western standards as trained gynecologists? The goal is to provide girls with safe, trained, community counselor/workers or church mothers, not only to provide inspection but accountability to the young girls, as well as someone in whom to confide. Virginity testing for girls is not the sole solution to HIV/AIDS. This would make HIV/AIDS a women's issue—as if they were the only ones responsible for the transmission of the virus, especially when it is spread through sexual intercourse. Men and boys who are spreading the disease through unprotected sex, rape, and abuse of girls and women need to be held accountable as well. In addition, we have to understand that HIV/AIDS does not discriminate based on gender. Boys play an equal role, if not a greater role, in being sexually responsible. It is older men of these communities who must aim at being good role models.

23 Associated Press, "AIDS Testing Recommended for Most Americans."

What about Boys?

Traditionally, uncles and grandfathers were crucial in teaching boys about young adulthood and the "not openly spoken of subjects" of sex and sexuality. Michael Gelfand says about the role of grandparents and uncles in the education of boys who are between twelve and sixteen, at the age of puberty:

> At this age, children are taught the meaning of marriage, and their education towards this end extends over several years. The grandfather (maternal or paternal) is responsible for the sex education of his grandsons and for warning them to keep their purity until they marry. Every now and then, he is supposed to warn them about this. He says, "If you are caught doing the sexual act, we shall take you to the chief to have your penis cut off" [This was to ward the boys from misbehaving since there are no known instances where a boy's penis was cut for impregnating a girl.] If a boy is seen in the company of girls, the grandfather repeats the warning. The aim is to have a fine marriage for each boy and girl. Boys are warned that from puberty onwards, male sex urges become aroused but they must be controlled and correct behavior is expected of them. They are watched as well as informed.[24]

The above were sex-education practices, which have died in the cities but are still practiced in some parts of the country. Many children in the city are left at the mercy of the TV or other peers for their education on these crucial matters since both parents might be busy trying to make a living.

There is no denying that Africa is still a very patriarchal society. Over the years, and even today, the responsibility about sex has always been laid on the mothers and the daughters. If a girl becomes pregnant, it is the girl and the mother who are to blame. In another article, Chimedza writes about this inequality in how women are treated as opposed to men, who are infected with HIV. Usually the blame falls on women, while men are absolved from responsibility for their actions in contracting the disease. Even in cases where the man might have brought the infection home, sometimes the blame is placed on to the woman. Chimedza writes:

---

24. Gelfand, *Growing Up in Shona Society*, 17.

The impact of HIV and AIDS on women is particularly acute. In many developing countries, women are often economically, culturally and socially disadvantaged and lack equal access to treatment, financial support and education. In a number of societies, women are mistakenly perceived as the main transmitters of sexually transmitted diseases and HIV. HIV-positive women are treated very differently from men in many societies. Men are likely to be "excused" for their behavior that resulted in their infection, whereas women are not. A woman who brought her son to my medical practice for treatment was very bitter with her daughter in law, " . . . my son is a saint, but his wife is evil. It's because of her that my son got this disease". These intense emotions have caused a lot of anguish to those women perceived to be guilty of spreading the virus.[25]

In this day and age, it is time for fathers to hold their sons accountable and to train the boys to be sexually responsible. The responsibility in stopping the spread of HIV/AIDS lies squarely in the hands of both males and females. The age of "boys will be boys" is over, and we have to face the reality of the pandemic in our midst.

In many African communities, especially in the cities, boys are learning about sexuality based on what they see on TV or through other media. This leads children to experiment without any proper guidance, due to a lack of mentors and traditional ceremonies that used to be in place. Father figures need to train and remind the boys that the number of women with whom one has sex does not garner him recognition as a "real man." Rather, a real man is recognized in being responsible and accountable, especially when it comes to sexual behavior.

We need to teach our children, (especially the boys), that having sex does not equal being a real man or woman. In addition, sex is not synonymous with love; love is an emotion. The media has confused our children that having sex is equal to "making love." True love is not made out of sexual intercourse. Self-respect, respect for others and being responsible is more honorable than bragging about with how many women one had sexual intercourse. Some times as parents we are embarrassed to talk to our children about sex but then complain when what the media teaches is against our values or growl and mourn when the teens try to find out on their own. Most of the youth already know about this material from school or from the media; however,

25. Chimedza, "Stigma, Discrimination Dangerous."

what they need from us is the right application of the information. Most parents won't comment on bad sexualized com-
mercials or TV shows when something inappropriate comes on.
This is the time for parents to teach their children what is wrong
or right about the sexualized scenes.[26]

The traditional practices of initiation-to-manhood ceremonies
need to be reclaimed as part of sex education. It is during these events
that the boys need to be educated about sexual responsibility in general
and the issues of HIV/AIDS specifically. With each passing generation, there are some practices that need to continue in order to lay the
foundations for the next generation, and there are some that need to
be dropped for the sake or betterment of future generations. The two
traditions highlighted above (female virginity testing and male initiation rites) need to continue, and practices such as confidentiality need
to be reassessed or applied differently.

In conclusion, there is much politics involved between Western
countries and indigenous contexts in working with the HIV/AIDS infected, especially what pertains to drug research and patents. The ethics
of whether the pandemic must be treated as a public-health issue instead
of a human-rights issue needs to be reconsidered. The ethical values of
the Shona are contrary to Western ones imposed by the medical system
when the pandemic was first discovered. It is not only through sexual
contact that people are dying from the pandemic. In indigenous contexts, especially in Africa, traditional practices on sex education need
to be revived as a way to fight against the HIV/AIDS pandemic. Even in
cases where the infection is due to sexual contact, there are other factors needing consideration, such as poverty and poor medical systems.
The next chapter presents the issues of a culture of death created by
combination of poverty and the HIV/AIDS pandemic.

26. Mucherera, "Hope in the Midst of Struggle," 92–93.

3

A Culture of Death

Poverty and HIV/AIDS

The hand of the Lord came upon me and he brought me
out by the spirit of the Lord and set me down in the middle
of a valley; it was full of bones. He led me around them; there
were very many lying in the valley, and they were very dry.
He said to me, "Mortal can these bones live?" I answered,
"O Lord God, you know." . . . They say, "Our bones are dried
up, and our hope is lost; we are cut off completely."

(Ezekiel 37:1–3, 11b)

When Death Is All Around Us: The Valley of Death

"Urombo uroyi hunoparadza" is a Shona saying that means,
"Poverty is poison; it kills or destroys." Poverty and HIV/AIDS have
proven to be deadly partners in causing horrendous evil all around the
world. The combination of poverty, a dead economy, the HIV/AIDS
pandemic, plus the collision of cultures, has caused much suffering and
havoc in many indigenous contexts, especially in Zimbabwe. Even before
the age of HIV/AIDS, poverty everywhere has always been one of the
worst enemies to humanity. The mixture of poverty and HIV/AIDS is a
sure death sentence to poor people. In this chapter, I introduce some of
the major indigenous contexts such as Africa face, with major reference
to Zimbabwe. The problems introduced here are not the only ones, but
are among the major contributing factors to the suffering of the people

of Zimbabwe. I do realize that the issues presented in this book may be more complicated than the way they are stated; however, common sense will show that the issues presented are key to the overwhelming suffering experienced in Zimbabwe. The main problems noted are poverty and a poor economy due to corruption, HIV/AIDS, and a collision of cultures. All these problems are interrelated, and their combination has produced bleak conditions for the people and for the future of the country. Case studies will illustrate the problems Zimbabwe is facing. The following example from my own firsthand experience shows the suffering taking place due to poverty and HIV/AIDS.

In 2004 I was home in Zimbabwe with my mother. She told me that one of our neighbors we were very close to, Mai Madube, had just died of AIDS. Growing up, I had known both this woman and her husband as a very strong, dedicated Christian couple. When my mother told me she had died of AIDS, my response was, "She couldn't have died of AIDS; they were a very strong Christian couple; one wouldn't expect this from such a couple." My mother looked at me with disbelief. She read my mind. She said, "Even strong Christians with good values are dying of AIDS, my son. You have been in America too long; you read, see, and believe all the lies they tell you on TV that all people in Africa are dying of AIDS because of extramarital sex and sexual promiscuity. Yes, there are some who are dying because of these affairs, but that is not the whole story. I don't know how many people we have buried so far, who died of HIV/AIDS, who did not engage in these behaviors at all." She went on to say that Mai Madube did not die of AIDS because she engaged in extramarital affairs; her husband did not either. "She did not die of AIDS," my mother said, "but died of poverty and a mother's love."

"You see, Mai Madube's son, Tatenda, contracted HIV/AIDS. How? Nobody seems to know. Tatenda had a big open bleeding wound on his foot that would not heal. The mother had to dress this wound every day. Some people told her she would get AIDS because she was touching the open wound with her bare hands. She knew about gloves, but because of poverty she could not afford to buy gloves. Madube's family had to think of putting food on the table first before they could think about buying gloves. Others even wondered how she had a stomach not to loathe and be averse to taking care of her son, who had a wound that smelled like gangrene—a situation many believed he brought on himself.

"Mai Madube vowed that as long as her son lived, she would love him and treat him like a person. She did not want him to experience a lonely death because of this horrendous disease. She took care of her son for almost six months, and it is during that time she contracted the disease. She had some blisters that opened up from weeding her garden, and yet she had continued to take care of Tatenda. She washed her hands all the time, as is the advice, but she still caught the disease. "For us who knew Mai Madube and have seen this type of thing happening many times, Mai Madube did not die of AIDS; she died of poverty and a mother's love."

My mother went on to share that at her age of seventy, she had never experienced such death and suffering as she had witnessed in these last two decades. "The person who invented HIV/AIDS will never enter heaven," she said. "This is the genocide of genocides, and he or she knew well to put HIV in poor countries where one can 'smell poverty,' where there is no medicines and the necessary material to take care of the infected. I think the person really wanted to wipe out all the poor people from the face of the earth so the rich can then come and take over the lands," she said. "When one walks the streets you meet all these young children without parents. Whoever thought a twelve-year-old 'with milk still coming out of his nose,' could be a head of a household? I pray to the Lord to put a stop to this unnecessary suffering."

The Poor and an Economy under Siege

The above conversation with my mother has stayed with me, and it helped me to ask tough questions as I traveled around the country doing workshops with pastors on issues of HIV/AIDS. It is true there are people who are dying from having been infected by HIV because of infidelity or prostitution, and I will give examples of such situations as well. However, there are so many forgotten faces of women and children who have been innocently infected and affected. We usually don't hear about them since, as my mother said, the story we hear of from the "Western scientific research and media" is that most Africans who are dying of HIV/AIDS have acquired it through sexual means. Some even claim that the reason there is much spread of HIV in Africa, especially, is because Africans cannot control their sexual desires or urges. This is far from the truth. It is the combination of poverty and HIV that is continuing to produce horrendous suffering.

Poverty did not invent itself; it is a human creation. One looks around the world to find people who are literally dying of obesity while others in a bordering country are dying or starving because they cannot find a little piece of bread to make it through the day. Due to poverty, there is malnutrition, lack of medication, and poor health-care systems. In many of the developing countries around the world, people are dying from diseases that could easily be treated elsewhere. The poor suffer and die, while the rich and their government officials can drive or fly across borders to get health care and everyday commodities.

In an indigenous context such as Zimbabwe, it is not only those who are HIV/AIDS infected who are crying out, as did the children of Israel during Ezekiel's period of prophecy (Ezek 37:1–3, 11b), but it is also those who are affected. If it is not HIV/AIDS killing the people; it is the poor economy and drought conditions; if it is not the economy and drought, it is the collision of cultural values destroying and breaking down the traditional family social structural support systems, causing misery each and every day. Many people in the country of Zimbabwe are losing hope, and others have literally left the country to seek greener pastures or simply survival. Others are praying and asking the question, why are people continuing to suffer under such conditions while other humans, and God, are watching and not coming to their aid? "Why, God?" they ask, "Is there hope in the current African country of Zimbabwe?" The country has become the valley of death, with not much relief in sight. There are little glimmers of hope, and yet the picture of the future seems to be getting gloomier.

It is generally agreed that it takes about one US $1 per day to feed each hungry child from developing countries of the world. We have people with billions of dollars sitting in their bank accounts (waiting for a rainy day) while children are dying for a piece of bread. The world is watching, and there is plenty to go around, but the contagious disease of global greediness continues. At the local level in Zimbabwe, we have similar occurrences of greediness and selfishness. The government itself set up an anticorruption commission because of corrupt leaders.

> The government of Zimbabwe has demonstrated its resolve
> and political will to effectively combat corruption through the

creation of the Ministry of State Enterprises, Anti-Corruption & Anti-Monopolies. The ministry is dedicated to fight corruption through systems of integrity that ensure transparency and fairness both in the private and public sectors. The Ministry is charged with the responsibility of fighting corruption that impedes economic and social development and monitor restrictive practices and unfair business practices especially the trends in mergers and acquisitions. The ministry also administers the Anti-Corruption Commission Act 2004, which provides for the setting up of the Anti-Corruption Commission. The Anti-Corruption Commission is an independent, powerful and high profile body, which provides mechanisms to investigate corruption at all levels in Zimbabwe.[1]

We can't keep blaming the West for all the suffering in the country without paying attention to the corruption occurring under our noses in this country. Corruption is destroying the economy. No one wants to invest in a country where corruption is rampant. Even the president, Robert Mugabe, himself has recognized it. Recently, he was quoted in the state run newspaper:

President Mugabe has castigated some senior Zanu-PF [Zimbabwe National Union-Patriotic Front] officials who were abusing their authority to amass properties and wealth, saying the ruling party might be forced to embark on a campaign to weed them out. Addressing the 66th Ordinary Session of the Zanu-PF Central Committee at the ruling party's headquarters in Harare yesterday, Cde Mugabe said some senior party officials were abusing their authority by acquiring wealth for self-aggrandizement. The President said some were seeking to evict ordinary people who had been legally allocated farms while others were demanding first preference in the allocation of business stands or houses built under Operation Garikai. "We shall now be bound to have a campaign of cleansing the Central Committee. You are not being fair; the numbers are growing. Some of you are being crookish even in leadership positions."[2]

The gap between the poor and the rich keeps widening each day, the dollar value tumbles, inflation is soaring, and the prices of everyday commodities skyrocket. To use my mother's words, one can "smell

1. Ministry of State Enterprises, Anti-Corruption & Anti-Monopolies Ministry Profile, "Fight Corruption."

2. "No to Abuse of Power."

poverty." In fact, most of the people can no longer afford the basic commodities of bread and milk.

> Bread is now a luxury to many families after retailers increased its price again. . . . Workers at a city bakery attributed the sharp increase to the price of wheat, which rose from $900 000 a ton to more than $12 million. The Grain Marketing Board is buying wheat from farmers at about $6 million a ton. "That is the only way we can remain viable because the price of wheat was also increased. There are also chances of the bread prices being increased again before the end of the year," said a worker who requested anonymity. Efforts to get a comment from the National Bakers Association chairman, Mr. Burombo Mudumo, were fruitless as he was said to be out of office.
>
> However, residents who spoke to Chronicle said bread was now beyond their reach and they would now have to do without it. "I have since stopped buying bread because it is quite expensive. It is better to have isitshwala (thick porridge) in the morning than to have bread and tea," said Mr. Mehluli Ncube.
>
> President Mugabe last week lambasted profiteers for scuttling the Government's efforts in turning around the fortunes of the economy.[3]

In this circumstance, no one is going to think about buying gloves if they are taking care of someone who is HIV infected. If one cannot even afford to buy bread and milk, how could one even think about buying basic health-care materials? Again, it is not just a question of immorality that HIV/AIDS has spread like wildfire in Sub-Saharan Africa and in most of the indigenous poor countries; HIV/AIDS has just added fuel to the fire that was already burning. As I argued earlier, before HIV/AIDS showed up on the scene, poverty was there, and it had already killed many people.

The Zimbabwean government made things worse also by allowing illegal land invasions. Much productive farmland is just laying unfarmed. This worsened the economic situation in Zimbabwe. The land issue in Zimbabwe is complicated, but at the same time, the government, from year 2000, mishandled the situation for the sake of buying votes. Land was given to people who did not have the means, and some knew little about how to farm the land. Other people ended up with two or more farms (lying in waste) while others did not get any land.

---

3. Chitemba, "Bread Prices Go Up Again."

In other words, some of the economic crisis was self-created by those who drove away the farmers (especially by those who drove away some of the white farmers) who were being very productive.

The Ugly Face of Poverty: Prostitution and "Small Houses"

Today, with more women finding their way into the city to work, some reach for the old trade of prostitution to make ends meet. The situation has worsened with the very poor economy and with the heads of households dead from the HIV/AIDS pandemic. Many times people miss the point that what is forcing these young women or single mothers into prostitution is poverty. I remember that one prostitute interviewed on Zimbabwean television, when asked why she was into prostitution and if she was afraid of catching HIV and dying from AIDS replied, "Which way is not dying, dying of hunger or dying of AIDS? I have been doing this for some time now, and I am still alive. I would rather die of AIDS than die of hunger." This does not justify this woman's behavior or thinking processes, but it says much about what poverty can force people to do. The economic crisis in the country has caused people to resort to lifestyles worse than ever thought of before. In another situation, a single mother was noted as saying that she would rather die of HIV/AIDS while trying to feed her children than to watch her children die of hunger.

The situation in Zimbabwe has created a culture of death. Some see this culture of death mentality slipping into the minds of the younger generation. You hear some of the youth say such statements as, "I might as well enjoy myself since death is just around the corner." I remember watching an interview on TV of a prostitute in Harare. When she was asked whether she used condoms to protect herself from being infected with HIV, her response was, "Have you ever eaten sweets [candy] in their wrapper? Why would I want it that way? If I am going to have sex, then I am not going to have that plastic [condom]; I want to enjoy it." For this woman, enjoyment was more important than to be alive.

As I stated earlier, we have two main groups of people in Zimbabwe today: the very rich and the very poor. The rich are exploiting the poor, and the poor have nowhere to turn other than to self-abuse or to literally sell themselves to those who have. There is no way one would look at some of the scenarios that have developed in Zimbabwe today and not point a finger to poverty. A new phenomenon has developed in Zimbabwe called the "small house." This is where a man will have two women, the wife at home and another—a mistress—living in another part of the city. The mistress or girlfriend has been nicknamed the "small house." In the West, this phenomenon is known as having an affair outside of marriage.

Some of the women (mistresses) who are willing to be involved in the "small house" lifestyles are those who are trying to make ends meet economically. However, others do it as professional prostitutes. For some, the husband's death forces them into these situations in order to maintain the family—they have mouths to feed and no other means to make a living. In some situations, women are forced by their bosses to compromise their values in order to cater to the welfare of the family. At the end of the day, the sad story is that some of these bosses, or rich men, end up infecting these women with HIV, since they usually have many sexual partners. They are to blame in many instances where the wives of these bosses also die of HIV/AIDS. There have been several court cases reported of wives beating or stabbing a "small house" mistress, and then literally hanging herself afterwards. The following are examples of stories from local newspapers in Zimbabwe.

> Yesterday, Mateyo appeared before Justice Yunus Omerjee, charged with murder. Mateyo, however, denied the charge, arguing that she had no intention of killing Lembani when she stabbed her in the heat of the moment. Mateyo claimed Lembani had incensed her after she caught her red-handed emerging from a nearby bush accompanied by her husband. She admitted that she knew about the affair before the tragedy. "When I asked my husband to explain where he was coming from with her, he rudely responded. Lembani, who earlier on had several times vowed to continue with the affair, was also provocative to me," she said. Venrandah Munyoro, for the State, however urged the court to convict Mateyo of murder with actual intent, arguing that she had planned to physically eliminate Lembani over the alleged infidelity. While cross-examining Mateyo, Munyoro said the accused had threatened to kill Lembani before she finally delivered the fatal blow. "I put it to you that you actually planned the murder. You went to her (Lembani's) house screaming at the top of your voice that you would murder her, which you later did," the prosecutor submitted. . . . The tragic

case comes against the background of a concerted campaign by the political hierarchy, with Vice-President Joice Mujuru lashing out at the proliferation of "small houses", a street term used to refer to mistresses. There is a growing trend of cases involving cheating husbands. Most of the cases end up in violence and sometimes in the death of one of the partners.[4]

The situation of the "small houses" or "affairs" has even become a concern for the government. What I see as a problem here is that the government is focusing on the behaviors rather than what is causing this type of activities to persist. The economic situation is the main problem that is resulting in some of these women's engaging in this conduct. It does not mean that the problem of "small houses" will totally be eradicated even with a better economy, but it will be much less prevalent and probably left mainly to those who lead the life of prostitution. Another local newspaper, the *Chronicle*, reports this "small house" incident that happened in Victoria Falls.

> In a fit of rage, a well known Victoria Falls businesswoman allegedly severely assaulted and stripped naked her husband's "small house," after catching the lovebirds arm-in-arm. The two were coming from the mistress's lodgings. The incident happened on Tuesday morning. Mrs. Menela Moyo, who runs restaurants, a bottle store and other businesses in the resort town, allegedly assaulted and tore off the clothes of one Mercy, whom she was accusing of going out with her husband. Sources said Moyo's husband had since moved out of the marital home and was staying with the mistress. Contacted for comment, Mrs. Moyo (38) admitted assaulting her husband's lover. She said the 20-year-old hairdresser had ruined her marriage since her 40-year-old husband had stopped fending for his family. "I got a tip-off that my husband was dating this girl and I decided to make investigations until I caught them. But what really pained me more was the fact that my husband is wasting the family wealth on her and only last month, he sold five of my beasts just to spend money on the girl," said the fuming Mrs. Moyo. The husband could not be reached for comment, as his phone was not reachable. Police in Victoria Falls confirmed the incident.[5]

4. "'Small House' Killed."
5. "Woman Strips 'Small House.'"

The few instances above are an indication that the issue of "small houses" has become an issue in destroying marriages as well as a problem in the spread of HIV. Men who do this can become a danger to the woman they are married to as well as to the "small house" woman in the spread of the disease.

> A 26-year-old Bulawayo woman hanged herself with an electrical cord after discovering that her husband had an extramarital affair, Chronicle learnt yesterday. . . . A relative of the deceased woman, who did not want her name to be disclosed, said the woman, Anna Ngwenya, of Gwabalanda suburb, hanged herself on Saturday night in the toilet of her matrimonial home while her husband was asleep. "The couple, which had two children, had been having serious domestic problems with the wife accusing her husband of being unfaithful," she said. "Things came to a head on Tuesday last week when the husband's 'small house' (girlfriend), with whom he has a child, visited the family. I am told that the husband spent two nights with the 'small house' in a spare bedroom ignoring his wife." The relative said that this infuriated the wife who threatened to beat up her husband's girlfriend. "As a result of the quarrel in the family, the girlfriend eventually left on Thursday, but the situation remained tense," she said. On Saturday night, the woman sneaked out of the bedroom and hanged herself. When the husband woke up at night, he realized that his wife was not there and he started searching for her. "He found her hanging in the toilet and alerted neighbors who reported the matter to the police."[6]

I am not arguing that all small houses will disappear as soon as the economy recovers. However, situations such as these have become so prevalent because of poverty and a bad economy. Sometimes people end up engaging in such behaviors to take care of their children; however, others are just simply trying to survive.

Another Ugly Face of Poverty: "Sugar Daddies"

Besides the situation of "small houses," we also have another problem—that of "sugar daddies." Usually these are rich men, many of them married, who cheat on their wives by privately having affairs with younger women. The key issue is they are rich and have money to literally pay

---

6. Chuma, "Woman Hangs Self over Small House."

the young girls to sleep with them. The intention of these men is not to marry the girls but just to have a "good time." Some pay the girls to have sex in return for payment of school fees, clothes, gifts, and other luxuries.

Due to poverty, many women and young girls who sleep with these men need money to survive and end up contracting the deadly virus. As stated earlier, many of the orphans who are left to fend for the family have the burden of making sure their younger brothers and sisters have food to eat. They are forced by the situation to enter into relationships with these "sugar daddies." A United Nations reporter interviewed one of these girls, Tracy Bunjwali:

> She's a sex worker, but not many passers-by would suspect that the slight figure standing in a narrow street opposite a nightclub in Zimbabwe's gold mining town of Kwekwe is also a university student. Tracy Bunjwali, a second-year business studies scholar and part-time prostitute, says her biggest fear is that she might bump into somebody she knows while out on the streets waiting to be taken to a nearby hotel-cum-brothel. She has little choice, she says. Orphaned during the last term of high school two years ago, the 23-year-old has to support a brother and sister still at school after her parent [*sic*] died of AIDS-related illnesses.
>
> Despite a government-run education assistance programme for vulnerable children and those orphaned by AIDS, the grant falls well short of needs in a country weighed down by triple-digit inflation. "My uncle, a municipal general hand, took us in when both our parents died, despite that he was struggling to feed, clothe, and send his own six children to school," Bunjwali said. "I don't come here often. I only do so when hard times befall the family," she explained. "I have to take the risk so that my brother and sister remain at school. . . . This is something I never imagined I would do," said Bunjwali. "I am aware of the risks and have decided to take a routine monthly visit to the voluntary counseling centre for an AIDS test." She has been tested three times so far, and all have been negative. "I have overcome the fear of visiting the centre," she added.[7]

If it were not for poverty and HIV/AIDS, one would not find a girl such as Tracy on the streets. She is taking this risk in order to take care of her brother and sister and to help them go to school. The parents' deaths left her as the breadwinner since the uncle's income could not

7. PlusNews, "ZIMBABWE: AIDS Orphans and Vulnerable Children."

support all of them. I pray that Tracy does not get infected, finishes school, and finds a job that will support the rest of the family. The added complication to her situation is that with the economy so bad, even if she were to graduate, it won't be easy for her to find a decent job to support herself, her brother, and her sister.

Tracy and her siblings were very fortunate that the uncle took them in, even though the uncle's income could not sustain them. Many of the children who are orphaned by HIV/AIDS end up on the street with the extended family leaving them to fend for themselves. This never used to be the case in this traditional indigenous culture.

A situation such as Tracy's is not isolated to a student who prostitutes to care for younger siblings. There are many reports of students at university campuses (both male and female) resorting to prostitution in order to make ends meet. The following is an example of such a report:

> First, students, like millions of their countrymen, are going hungry on campuses. Universities and colleges simply cannot provide enough food for them. The government is broke and the meager allowance it doles out to students is not enough to supplement the miserable food provided, let alone to buy books. Grant payments are frequently made months late because the government is cash-strapped and inefficient. Second, students feel they have to pass at all costs, even if it means sleeping around with lecturers. According to a social studies lecturer at Harare's University of Zimbabwe—where sexual harassment of women students is rife—this has turned the whole concept of manhood upside down. "Young women at campuses want men who can provide for them," she said. "They want men who can supplement the little food provided on campus. They want men who can take them to movies. They want men who can pay to have their hair done at the hairdressers. They want men who make them feel like ladies." Such men are known as "sugar daddies" and are deeply resented by other male students. The social studies lecturer recalled a tragic incident not so long ago when an impoverished female first-year undergraduate, Tecla Tom, committed suicide in a student hostel as an apparent way out of entrapment by a "sugar daddy". She left a note for her husband, which said in part, "It does not matter, Innocent, my husband, the time had come." When students subsequently went on the rampage against the hold of sugar daddies on women students, 20-year-old science undergraduate Batanayi Madzidzi was beaten up and killed by police.

The massive economic crisis gripping Zimbabwe—with inflation approaching 600 (now 1000) per cent and eighty per cent of the population living below the poverty line—has not spared the education system, and students are the chief victims of the malaise. . . . "Then there is the question of 'sex for exam and course work marks.'" "They will sleep with female students and pass them without any qualm," said the social studies academic. "Like everyone else, female students just want to get the hell out of university. They cannot contemplate being failed and having to spend another year at the institutions." So, she says, it is common practice for female students to have a sugar daddy as well as a regular boyfriend. After finishing college, they quickly want to erase the memory of the sugar daddy and marry the young boyfriend. "But sometimes it is not easy to make the transition from the sugar daddy to the boyfriend because the boyfriend is still a young man struggling to get his feet squarely on the ground," she continued. Nor are male students exempt from prostitution. They hang around with "sugar mummies"—older women who are either divorced or widowed but who have the means to maintain a "toy boy." "It is common for older women to drive into campus and pick up these young men. The situation is desperate," said the social studies lecturer. "Campuses have become the epicenters of the spread of diseases such as AIDS." The toy boys have become social misfits and rarely socialize with young women of their age. With AIDS rife in Zimbabwe, affecting an estimated quarter of the population aged 15 to 49, their sugar mummies are often HIV-positive, and the boys themselves are left to die lonely deaths from AIDS after the women have passed away."[8]

The crisis causing all of this is not HIV/AIDS; it is the economic crisis, which is affecting every corner of Zimbabwean society. People are being driven to these behaviors to make ends meet. The system of the extended family has also broken down. The nuclear-family system has replaced the extended family system, especially in the cities where people depend on income based on employment from blue-collar and industrial jobs. We face a culture of *mazvake mazvake*—meaning, "Each person for him- or herself and God for us all," or "Lift yourself up by your own bootstraps." In the age of poverty, it is the economically strong who are "running the show," even though the values they are using to run the show might be a death sentence to the community.

8. Unendoro, "Zimbabwean Students Driven to Prostitution."

Spare Them the Death Sentence: The Widow's and Girl-Child's Plight

There is definitely a need for many in the indigenous contexts to change some of the traditional practices, especially in the face of the HIV/AIDS pandemic. In the following few pages, I will address the issues of *nhaka* (widow inheritance) and *kuzvarira* (arranged marriages for girls while they are infants or children) as examples of traditions that need to change. These systems have become very dangerous, especially in the face of HIV/AIDS. They either need to be abolished or be revised to protect the widow and the girl. I will first give some background to the custom of *nhaka*. The focus here is in situations where the husband has died.

The concept of *nhaka* (widow inheritance), when put into proper perspective, was and is a very noble one. *Nhaka* was established so that no child or children would be left orphaned. The system was also established so that no widow would be left to struggle alone, raising her children by herself without extended family support. Usually families were big (about eight children per family), and the widow had many mouths to feed. Having a man from the immediate family in charge of helping raise the boys into manhood was an added benefit. The boys would have a male figure to look to, and all the children were not left as orphans without a father figure or male role model. Even in situations where a female was the one to take the traditional role of husband, there were male figures from the community for the boys as role models. The system was also put in place to protect orphans from abuse, especially sexual. *Nhaka,* in and of itself, is not a bad system; however, there are men who are abusing the system.

Traditionally, and in many instances, women were not forced into these relationships. The woman was given the choice to go back to her family of origin if she was still very young, and if no children were born of the marriage. If the young woman chose to go back, however, her family of origin was forced to pay back some of the dowry. If children had been born through the marriage, it was common for the widow to choose to stay to take care of her children. In some circumstances, however, if a brother of the deceased was interested in the widow, there were cases where the widow was forced either to compromise and marry him or to leave the family. Again, many women chose to stay for the sake of their children.

As much as the intentions of the *nhaka* custom were to help the widow and the orphaned children, many men began abusing the system for sexual advantages. It is frightening that even in situations where a widow (whose husband is known to have died of HIV/AIDS complications), some men are accepting the custom of *nhaka* with the intentions of having sexual relationships with the widow. The following comes from my firsthand experience of this type of situation when I traveled back to Zimbabwe in 2004.

Is This Real? What is He Thinking?

I had gone to the funeral of one of our retired pastors, at a church where I had also served as pastor. Many people wanted to speak with me when they heard I was around. Among these was a woman in her early sixties. (I will call her Mrs. Jonasi.) As soon as she found me, she was in tears, sobbing. Since we were at a funeral, I just took it that she was moved by emotions because of the loss the pastor. I, therefore, tried to console her, focusing on the death of the pastor. She stopped crying and then told me that the reason she was crying was not because of the pastor's death. She explained that as soon as she heard I was around, she started looking for me because she believed I was the only person who could help her, and to whom her husband would listen. "What seems to be the problem?" I asked.

This is what she shared. Mrs. Jonasi husband's younger brother (that is, Mrs. Jonasi's brother-in-law) had died about six months before. Before his illness, he had been the manager of a big firm, and the company was paying for the children's school fees. When he died, the doctors wrote on the death certificate the cause of death as "pneumonia, TB and HIV-related complications." The brother-in-law had been sick for about five months, being in and out of the hospital. He left three children. Mrs. Jonasi said she had noticed that the widow's (her sister-in-law's) health had started deteriorating in the last three months of her husband's illness. She (the widowed sister-in-law) had not gone in to be tested to see whether she was HIV positive, but Mrs. Jonasi suspected she was. At this point, Mrs. Jonasi started to cry uncontrollably. I sat there until she calmed down.

She then said that her husband had officially been given the right to widow inheritance by the extended family. Mrs. Jonasi thought that since her husband was a Christian, he would accept the role, but only to help the deceased family without engaging in a sexual relationship with the widow. She mentioned that there had been many different times when Mr. Jonasi had come home very late indicating he had been at the widow's house. Mrs. Jonasi also indicated that she and her husband had ceased to be sexually intimate, and that Mr. Jonasi had not shown any interest in her in this area of their life lately. She said that it was a "God thing" that he was no longer interested because she would not have known how to say no if he had insisted that they become sexually intimate—she had already become suspicious.

Mrs. Jonasi said she was afraid of being tested and believed it would make things worse for her if she found out she was positive. She said she would rather not find out since she had not experienced any changes in her health, and she would rather live with the hope that she was not HIV positive and place her focus instead on caring for her children. I asked Mrs. Jonasi whether she had sought any counseling with their pastor on these issues. She told me no. She said they had a woman pastor, and her husband had no respect for women pastors. "He won't even give her an ear if she were to come to speak to us," she said. I asked Mrs. Jonasi about whether she had noticed any changes in the husband's health. She said yes, there were some changes in that he had been experiencing some unusual headaches in the last two months, which he never used to have. I told Mrs. Jonasi I would try to see her husband while at the funeral, but told her the chances were slim that we would be able to talk much about these deep relational issues for which she was asking help. I then prayed with Mrs. Jonasi.

When I opened my eyes, I saw Mr. Jonasi from a stone's throw, coming in our direction. Mrs. Jonasi waited until he got near, and then she bid me goodbye and left me to talk to Mr. Jonasi. As soon as she left, three other men who had come to greet me sat down beside me. I did not get the chance to be alone with Mr. Jonasi until it was time for us to leave for the burial ceremony. I then returned to Harare where I was staying. After a week, I left Zimbabwe for the USA and never got the chance to talk to Mr. and Mrs. Jonasi, and do not know what became of them.

I think of Mrs. Jonasi often, wondering how many other women are in her predicament. The main issue has to do with a tradition that used to be noble, but now has *death* written all over it. This is one of the traditions that needs to be reassessed or dropped for the sake of this and the next generation's survival. If a woman is forced into *nhaka* (being inherited in marriage) by a man whose wife died of AIDS, the disease ends up killing not only the man, but also his wife and the widow, leaving the children as orphans. We are knowingly giving these women a death sentence by sanctioning a tradition that sends death into their home. As stated above, some men will take the vow of *nhaka* for the sake of getting sexual access to the widow. Oliver Mutukudzi is one of the most renowned singers and social analysts in Zimbabwe. He sang a song condemning the men who are abusing this system of widow inheritance (*nhaka*), reminding them that their behavior runs against the grain of the initial intention of the custom.[9] The song says, "Nhaka sandi bonde, nhaka kuriritira mhuri yasiwa nemufi," translating to, "The purpose of [widow] inheritance is not for the sake of sleeping with the widow, nor for the man to have the right to sex, but for the sake of taking care of the orphaned family."

Traditionally, in its time, the practice was a very noble one; it ensured that the wife and children of the deceased were not left without a breadwinner. In today's age of HIV/AIDS, it might be a time to reassess the function of *nhaka* and try to protect the vulnerable women who choose not to enter into this type of traditional practice. In short, it is the communities' job to protect these women and save them from the death sentence.

Poverty and Girl-Child Marriages

Due to poverty, there are recent increases in the marriage of the *girl-child*. The tradition of marrying the infant girl-child *kuzvarira* (before she is even weaned from the mother's breast), and *kuputsira* (a family's marrying off a young girl-child) are reported to be on the increase in Zimbabwe. The dangers of the girl-child being married to an HIV/AIDS- positive man and being infected are increasingly high since

---

9. Mutukudzi, "Sandi Bonde." On the same album, *Paivepo*, Mutukudzi also has a song in which he says that in this day and age of HIV/AIDS there are some men (womanizers) who are just lucky to be alive.

some of these rich men who usually end up marrying the girl-child do not remain faithful. According to the following newspaper report, girl-child marriages have become a common occurrence.

> Tariro Muchina was barely in her teens late last year when her father "sold" her off into an arranged marriage in the small-scale farming district of Nyamajura, about 250km east of the Zimbabwean capital, Harare. Twelve months down the line, the 14-year-old Muchina, who was literally dragged screaming all the way into "marriage", appears to have come to terms with her fate. "I had to leave school to marry this man despite his age . . . My father insisted that I do it to save my younger brothers and sisters from hunger," Muchina says, opening up only after much persuasion. Muchina is married to a balding and pot-bellied 65-year-old man who has some teeth missing but owns a grocery shop—an immensely important factor in this hunger- and poverty-stricken community. Showing surprisingly little bitterness for someone robbed of her youth in so cruel a manner, Muchina sums up her story in just a few sentences. She says: "I would have preferred to continue with school. But we are poor and there was no money for food or anything at home. Although it [the marriage] was arranged for me, I had to agree to it. That is the only way my family could survive. In turn, my husband provides food for them."
>
> Faced with starvation after six years of poor harvests, Zimbabweans are resorting to centuries-old traditions of "forced marriages", known in the local Shona language as "kuzvarira", for survival. The practice, which involves a father giving away his usually under-age daughter (without her consent) to a richer man in return for food and other economic support, had died over the past 100 years. But some hungry families from rural communities, far removed from the glare of human rights groups and the media, are reviving the old custom out of desperation to survive an unprecedented economic and food crisis, which critics blame as much on poor weather as on mismanagement by President Robert Mugabe's government. . . . "We are seeing an increase in forced and illegal marriages of poor young girls to rich old men over the past few years. This is a centuries-old tradition, which we had long forgotten," a former University of Zimbabwe vice-chancellor and a leading social scientist, Gordon Chavhunduka, says. He adds: "Such traditions where poor families marry off their under-age daughters to rich old men were rife before colonialism hundreds of years back. They died after colonialism. But they have now been revived in

the battle for survival." A village elder in Nyamajura, Kennias Mutuni, says cases like that of Muchina are being reported with increasing frequency in the area because of poverty. But in a very worrying sign, the village elder sees little wrong with the old custom as long as the bride price is paid. "As long as the bride price is paid, that is fine with us. People want to survive and daughters, especially young and well-behaved ones, can be an avenue out of starvation," says Mutuni. And, rather cynically, he adds: "It is a legitimate way of forging relations between the rich and the poor so that they can take care of each other. It's better than losing the girls to prostitution." . . .

Eunice Chipfatsura, a pastor with a local Pentecostal church in Nyamajura, says there are no easy solutions to the problem, not least because community leaders, who are invariably men, still believe the males have a right to determine the future of female members of a family. Chipfatsura says: "It is difficult to make any headway. When we try to talk to the community leaders or even the children, they don't understand us. We were chased away in one village after encouraging the girl children to report such cases to the police. We have an uphill task because as the economy gets worse, the abuse of young girls sold like commodities will get worse as well. We need to get the message to the children, that it is abuse of their rights and they can report it." But for Muchina and probably many like her, the concern is not about human rights and dignity. It is, as the cliché goes, about bread-and-butter issues. "If I report to the police, will that bring food to my family?" she asks when told about the church pastor's advice that young girls like her should not accept being forced to marry men old enough to be their fathers but should instead inform the police.[10]

In the story above, the child has become content and asks the hard question: "Even if I were to report to the police, would that bring food to my family?" Poverty is at the root of the resuscitation of many traditional practices. The sad part of the whole situation is that the rich men who end up marrying these young girls have money and access to other women. They, therefore, end up infecting these innocent children because "they have money." The combination of poverty and HIV/AIDS has become very deadly for many women and girls in Africa, reinstating long-discarded traditions. The above examples are but a few of the

10. ZimOnline, "Girl-Children Sacrificed into Marriage."

traditional practices that are prescriptions for death sentences to many of the women and girls in parts of the African continent.

As we have seen, the culture of death in Zimbabwe today has been created by many factors, such as poverty, changes in traditions, and sometimes holding on to traditions that are deadly in this age of HIV/AIDS. I have argued that the high death rates in most indigenous contexts, and especially in Zimbabwe, are not solely based on the one factor of sexual promiscuity. It is the combination of poverty, poor health systems, corruption, and the HIV/AIDS pandemic that is causing the rise in the death toll. There is also need for the African community to reassess some of the African traditional values and practices, such as widow inheritance and marriages of girl children. These traditional practices are a death sentence to many of the women and girls involved.

In the next chapter, I address the question of whether there is any hope in these indigenous and/or African contexts. What are some of the circumstances that bring hope to the people of this indigenous context even in such a gloomy situation? Physical wounds leave a mark whilst psychological and spiritual wounds are embedded deeply, as internal cuts not visible to the eye, but that people carry throughout lives. These stories of pain must be shared in a healing manner, at the palaver, in order that their oppressive powers perpetuating psychological scarring from generation to generation can be usurped. The signposts of hope in these contexts are the African people's religion, efforts to revillage, and the reauthoring of their life stories.

4

Signposts of Hope

Religion, Revillaging, and Reauthoring

"Tariro yedu iri muna Dandemutande gawi rakatandirandira
nyika, iye Chidzachopo, Mwari wedu, Musikavanhu!"
("Our hope is in the One, the Web that surrounds the world,
the One found in Existence, the Ancient of Days, the Ageless one,
and the Creator, He Who Is, who created all of us humans!")

—Mbuya Tracy Mucherera

"Varume ndevamwe, kutsva kwendebvu vanodzimurana."
("'Men [humans] are all the same; when their beards burn they
help each other to extinguish the fire.' Men should show a spirit
of cooperation and sympathy. They should help one another in
times of difficulty and danger. . . . It also serves as a reproach for
people who are reluctant to give a hand to those who need it."[1])

—Shona proverb

THE HOPES OF the African peoples lie in God and humanity—that is, in
their religion, in revillaging, and in the reauthoring of their life stories
from subjugation to hope. The African people of Zimbabwe believe
that the story of humanity begins, is lived out, and ends with God. In
this chapter, we will look at the African people's unwavering hope in
God under excruciating pain and bitter suffering, and the hope brought
about by the realization of the power of revillaging and by the reauthoring of their story. How can a people be hopeful in a God who seems

---

1. Hamutyinei, *Tsumo-Shumo*, 39.

to be an onlooker, where thousands of people are being buried each month due to the HIV/AIDS pandemic and poverty? Could it be that the key elements to their hope is in the knowledge that this God, who seems to be an uninvolved observer of their travail, is an ardent participant and an ever-abiding presence in the midst of the circumstances of their suffering? Africans believe that humans were created to be in relationship not only with God but also with each other as well. Thereby hope is encountered from two fronts: primarily from God, who created humanity to be in relationship with God and, likewise, from one another in relationship.

In different indigenous contexts there are many creation stories similar to the ones recorded in the book of Genesis, making it easy for the Shona to resonate with the biblical creation story. In the first account of the creation (Genesis 1), after having created everything, God sees that "everything . . . was very good" (Gen 1:31). In the second account, it is only after God creates a man (Adam) that God says, "it was not good," because "it was not good for the man [Adam] to be alone" (Gen 2:18). God, therefore, created another being (Eve) so they could be in a relationship.

Another biblical concept is that humanity is charged with the responsibility of being a steward—naming the animals and all creation. In the first creation story, it is only humanity that is created in the *image of God*. It is of primary importance that humanity was and is created in God's image; thus, man and woman can relate to God, and vice versa. This does not mean that God could not exist without humanity, but rather that God created humanity for relationships.

A Theology of Life

As we continue in the story of Genesis, when humanity breaks relationship with God, it breaks God's heart. In fact, there would be no human story without God and humanity. The field of play for all humanity's activity is centered on God's creative and loving relationship with them. I borrow the idea from narrative counseling theory that humans' "landscape of identity" and "landscape of action" are highly influenced by their environments and their immediate relations.[2] Humanity, therefore, knows itself (its identity) through living life in relationship with

2. Morgan, *What Is Narrative Therapy?* 60ff.

God. The unfolding human drama (action) on earth effects and affects God's relationship with humanity. Among the Shona, this "field of play," or landscape, is in an environment where God is in loving control and is caring; yet at the same time, God has given humanity free will. Throughout life, individuals are in constant interaction with other humans, with all creation, and with God. Thus, humanity can only realize the fullness of their identity through, and in, God.

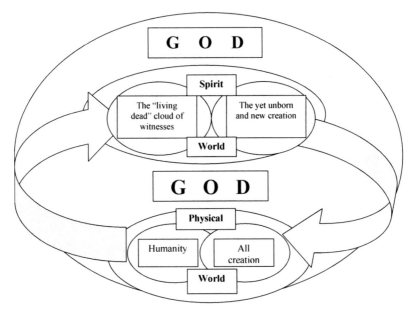

Figure 1   The Circle of Life

As Figure 1 ("The Circle of Life") indicates, life starts with God (spirit world), is lived out on this earth (physical world), and ends with God (spirit world). The Shona believe that in the unfolding of the "circle of life," God is at the center, as well as encompassing the circle. God surrounds, and is at, the creative center of the circle, sustaining humanity at every turn of life. The idea of the "cloud of witnesses" or the "living dead" as part of the spirit world is not found to be contrary to Christian beliefs. Jesus did talk about God as the "God of the living dead":

> And the fact that the dead are raised Moses himself showed,
> in the story about the bush, where he speaks of the Lord as the
> God of Abraham, the God of Isaac and the God of Jacob. Now

He is God not *of the dead*, but of the *living; for to him all of them
are alive.* (Luke 20:37–38, emphasis added)

So there is no reason to be without hope, for God is in the unfolding drama of life and in the center of human activities, redeeming
humanity. God is both at the center of and encompassing the spiritual
and physical space. The two, the spiritual and physical realms, are connected and evolve in God's sphere, and at the same time are under God's
control.

Attributes of Hope

As much as there are many instances where pain, suffering, injustice,
and any other form of evil seem to have taken center stage, the Shona
believe that God is still in loving control of that which God created.
God's being in control does not mean that evil or suffering will not
touch humans as a community or as individuals, but that God is present in those situations where evil and suffering exist. Evil and suffering,
therefore, will never overcome the goodness and loving nature of God
and God's love for humanity, since humanity was created out of God's
love. In the history of humanity, God has always restored order through
direct involvement, or by using a remnant when humanity has tried to
create chaos. Many Shona believe that suffering is temporal, but God is
eternal, and life with God is therefore eternal.

Religion for the Shona is part of everyday life. It is ingrained in
their upbringing, and is summed up in their saying, "to know and believe in God is to know life, and without God, one is as good as dead"
(Shona saying). Life must first and foremost evolve around the worship
of the Creator among them. Statements of some of the first missionaries
support this—that "Africans were notoriously religious."[3] For Africans,
one of the attributes of God is *Chidzachopo*. This attribute bears with it
two meanings: "one who was found in *existence*," and "one who is *ageless*, or the Ancient of Days." God is, therefore, the beginning of *life*, and
since God is ageless, humanity will spend eternity with God.

Another attribute of hope is found in the belief that the God who
is known as *Dandemutande gavi rakatandira nyika*, which translates as
"God who is as a spider web surrounding the whole world." In other

---

3. Mbiti, *African Religions and Philosophy*, 1.

words, there is no place where God is not; God is present everywhere, anytime. Another common saying among the Shona is, "Mwari ndewe vanhu wese." meaning, "God cares about the affairs of all—the poor, the widows, the orphans, the rich." In addition, it is believed that one does not need plenty to truly worship God and to have hope in God. For God is our utmost hope; God has never failed us. In most instances, the narrative one shares includes one's relationship both with God and with other humans here as well as those in the spirit world.

The Essence of Life: A Journey Never to be Walked Alone

In most indigenous contexts, there is much reliance on faith in the Creator and a great sense of interdependence with other individuals. To choose to go through life alone without the Creator, the family, and the wider community, is similar to choosing death, or to die a lonely death. The sense that one belongs has always been the key to African survival. Children are brought up with a belief that a person must "never walk the journey of life unaccompanied." To have life is to have one's story unfold in the midst of community. Individuals understand the fullness of their individual story through interpersonal relationships within their community of embeddedness. Essentially, a "theology of life" for most Africans is founded on their relationship with God, as well as their community. Day in and day out, we read about the rise in diseases, economic poverty, and wars in Africa. In the midst of all these catastrophes, the African peoples have never lost hope in their own survival. Those among the poorest of the poor still wake up to a new day with the hope that God will see them through that day.

For them, the greatest pain in this world emanates from being lonely, rejected, invisible, ignored, or, worse, separated from one's Creator. In indigenous contexts, especially among the Shona, besides physical death, one can experience emotional and relational death. Biblically speaking, the ultimate death for humanity is being separated from God. I agree with John Pobee, an African theologian, about what he sees as the difference between Western and African human existence: "Whereas Descartes spoke for Western man when he said *cogito ergo sum*—I think, therefore I exist—Akan (African) man's ontology is *cognatus ergo sum*—I am related by blood, therefore I exist, or I exist because I belong to a family . . . Family relationships determine the view of man."[4]

Humanity was created to live in community; therefore, the opening saying for this chapter: "Varume ndevamwe, kutsva kwendebvu vanodzimurana" ("Men [humans] are all the same; when their beards burn, they help each other to extinguish the fire. Thus, "Men should show a spirit of cooperation and sympathy. They should help one another in times of difficulty and danger."[5]) Humans were not created to live in isolation but to understand that what affects my neighbor is my problem as well.

Most Africans and other indigenous communities believe that the roots of an individual's personal identity are rooted in the community to which one belongs, thus the common saying, "I am because we are; since we are, therefore, I am."[6] Individuals see themselves in light of either the community to which they belong or their communal relationships. The saying, "It takes a village to raise a child," also points to the involvement of community in giving individuals an identity. There is no human who can survive as an island—without relationships.

Therefore, it follows, having been given one's identity by the community, that the stories one narrates are relationally based and unfold out of one's relationships. Individuals from indigenous contexts believe that persons are able to narrate the stories of pain, joy, or success based on the relationships that surround them. An African saying goes, "If you find a tortoise on a tree, it did not get there by itself." Whether one finds oneself in a situation considered good or bad, that individual did not get there alone. Any success we find ourselves experiencing in life must be celebrated with the community, and any downfall pains both the individual *and* the community.

Life in these communities is seen in terms of a triangle of relationships. These relationships help one understand who one is, and give one a sense of existence. Apart from these relationships, one cannot have a fully balanced identity. The following figure is an illustration of how people in these communities try to live out their theology, and how they understand their relationships.

4. Pobee, *Toward an African Theology*, 49.

5. Hamutyinei, *Tsumo-Shumo*, 39.

6. Mbiti, *African Religions and Philosophy*, 106.

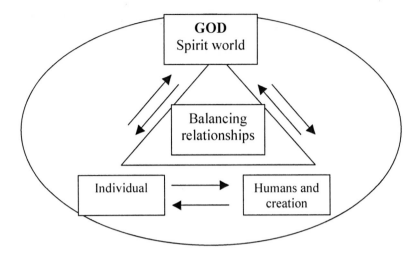

Figure 2   Communal Relationships: Theology of Life

In these indigenous contexts, communal relations are holistic, meaning that they include the living (all creation), the living dead (the cloud of witnesses), the spirit world, and God. Community, therefore, assumes all of life: the Creator (the spirit world included), the created, and those yet to come into existence. Life is perceived in a holistic manner, meaning that to have life is to have it in the broad understanding of the community. For most indigenous contexts, nothing can ring more true than the words of Mercy Oduyoye, an African theologian from Nigeria, when she describes creation stories and her definition of community. She says,

> In both African and Christian myths of origins, humankind becomes the center of the universe. But human beings wantonly exploit the world's physical and human resources to an extent that even God cannot tolerate . . . b). Related to the belief that humankind is the custodian of the earth is Africa's conviction that the past, present, and future generations form *one community*. Africans therefore try to hold in tension the demands of the traditions of the elders and the necessity to build for the future. Africans recognize life as life-in-community. We can truly know ourselves if we remain true to our community, both past and present. The concept of individual success or failure is secondary. The ethnic groups, the village, the locality, are crucial in one's estimation of oneself. Our nature as beings-in-relation is a two-way relation: with God and with our fellow human beings.

Expand the communal ideology of clans ad ethnic groups to nations and you have a societal system in which none is left in want of basic needs . . . c) A sense of *wholeness of the person* is manifested in the African attitude in life. Just as there is no separation between the sacred and the secular in communal life, neither is there a separation between the soul and the body in a person. Spiritual needs are as important for the body as bodily needs are for the soul.[7]

As Oduyoye states above, one's relationships with God, with humankind, and with all creation are important in the development of one's sense of self or of self-identity. When these relationships (with other humans, the Creator, or all of creation) are harmed, rituals are performed to right the wrong.

The Global Village: Supporting One Another's Falling Hands

African people in general, and the Shona people in particular, take seriously the idea that what affects my neighbor affects me. Interpersonal relations and interdependence form the bedrock of indigenous people's narratives and their sense of being. In these contexts, it is believed that the individuals within the community must never ignore or simply watch a neighbor struggle or suffer, because tomorrow the same struggle may turn to be theirs. Stories and proverbs are therefore shared (as cited above) to encourage people to work together. Life is a web of relationships that one has created. Each individual's story or life narrative spins and contributes to the "community's story."

From a biblical standpoint, I am reminded of the example given by Moses and Aaron in the battle against the Amalek. Exodus records: "So Joshua did as Moses told him, and fought with Amalek, while Moses, Aaron, and Hur went up to the top of the hill. Whenever Moses held up his hands, Israel prevailed; and whenever he lowered his hand, Amalek prevailed. But Moses' hands grew weary; so, they took a stone and put it under him, and he sat on it. Aaron and Hur held up his hands, one on one side and the other on the other side; so, his hands were steady until the sun set. And Joshua defeated Amalek and his people with the sword" (Exod 17:10–13). The battle became a community battle, and

---

7. Oduyoye, "Value of African Religious Beliefs," 110–11, italics original.

not just a battle for those who were at the battlefront or in the trenches, so to speak. Similarly the battle against HIV/AIDS and poverty involves all who live in the global village.

Pain and Suffering Know No National Boundaries

It is disheartening that as human beings in this global village, we are shying away from facing head-on the problems of poverty and HIV/AIDS with a united communal front. Communitarian theology must not be limited to indigenous contexts but must become the major guiding principle in eliminating the horrendous evils of poverty and HIV/AIDS. Due to the wars in the Middle East, world economies have been affected, and there is no country under the sun that has not suffered the side effects of these wars. Oil prices have skyrocketed everywhere, affecting transportation worldwide. The old adage "what goes around comes around" has proven true in our day and age. Diseases (such as HIV/AIDS) that started being perceived as only a homosexual, drug-user, poor-African–people's disease have found its way to heterosexuals, non–drug users, and the non-African rich. Until the global community realizes how much we need each other, and that what affects my neighbor ten thousand miles away may end up in my backyard, humanity will self-destruct, with thousands dying of hunger and HIV/AIDS each day.

In this age of the HIV/AIDS pandemic, of wars, and of economic interdependence, stories about the importance of community must take center stage to give hope to those who are suffering around the world. The problem of HIV/AIDS, though concentrated mostly to indigenous contexts, cannot be localized, especially with the increase in global mobility. Even though statistics indicate higher infection among indigenous communities (more so in sub-Sahara Africa), my argument is that problems such as HIV/AIDS know no national boundaries. The problem is a global one, and no person in any part of the world must think they are immune to being infected or affected. We as a global community must be driven by a theology that sees all humanity in this predicament, not just Africans, Asians, or Latinos. The pandemic is a world crisis, and it will take everyone to fight it.

"It Does Not Concern Me": A Shona Folktale about Community

A folktale is told among the Shona of Zimbabwe to remind people that any danger posed in the community is one that may affect many, even though it may not appear to do so initially. Pondering the devastating effects of HIV/AIDS in Zimbabwe, a colleague of mine, Rev. Geoffrey Kagoro, and I saw how true the following folktale is to our context and to the global village in general. The point in the folktale is that whenever someone recognizes something is posing a threat to or for the community, the whole community is to find ways to rid the community of the danger before it destroys everyone. We live in a world that seems to emphasize "each person is for himself or herself, and God for us all." We soon forget that as long as we are in the world, "we are in it together." We are together riding in the sinking ship; the water might not have reached my side of the ship, but soon I will also go down with the ship if I don't help stop the leak on your side.

> A story is told among the Shona people of a mouse that saw a rock trap set inside the king's house. The king's son had set a trap in the house to kill the mice. One of the mice went on to tell the rooster about the trap in the house and how the trap spelled danger to all of the tame animals belonging to this home.
>
> "Rooster, there is a trap in the house, that trap spells danger for all of us. We have to do something about the trap in the house."
>
> The rooster replied, "Have you ever seen a rooster under a trap or inside the house? That trap is set for you, idiot; you are the one who goes in the house. The trap has nothing to do with me whatsoever. It is none of my business. Leave me alone."
>
> As the mouse left, it said to the rooster: "Be forewarned, and remember this day that I told you the trap spells danger for all of us. We are community."
>
> "Not me, I don't look like a mouse and don't belong to your community of mice," the rooster responded.
>
> The mouse then went to the goat and said: "Goat, there is a trap in the house; that trap spells danger for all of us. We have to do something about the trap in the house."
>
> The goat replied, "Have you ever seen a goat under a trap or inside the house? That trap is set for you; you are the one who goes in the house. The trap has nothing to do with me whatsoever. It is none of my business. Leave me alone."

As the mouse left, it said to the goat: "Be forewarned, and remember this day that I told you the trap spells danger for all of us. We are community."

"Not me. I don't look like a mouse and don't belong to your community of mice," the goat responded.

The mouse left and went to the bull. As with the others, the mouse told the bull: "Bull, there is a trap in the house, that trap spells danger for all of us. We have to do something about the trap in the house."

The bull replied, "Have you ever seen a bull under a trap or inside the house? I can't even fit in the door of the house. That trap is set for you; you are the one who goes in the house. The trap has nothing to do with me whatsoever. It is none of my business. Leave me alone."

As the mouse left, it said to the bull: "Be forewarned, and remember this day that I told you the trap spells danger for all of us. We are community."

"Not me. I don't look like a mouse and don't belong to your community of mice," the bull responded.

As the mouse was running around in the yard, a snake saw it and pursued it. The mouse went into the house and the snake still followed. The mouse ran over the rock-trap, but the snake crawled right through the trap, and the trap fell on the snake, trapping half the body of the snake but not killing it. The king's son, who was playing outside, heard the trap fall and ran into the house. He did not notice the snake, and as he tried to lift the rock-trap, the snake bit the king's son.

The king heard the news, and he sent his son to the medicine person for treatment. He gave the rooster to the medicine person to be killed as food during the ritual of treatment. The mouse said to the goat and the bull, "I told you that trap spelled danger for all of us. There is the end of the rooster."

The son did not heal but continued to get worse. People started gathering at the king's house to support him when news arrived that the son's health was deteriorating. The king asked one of his servants to kill the goat to feed the many people now at the king's home. The mouse went to the bull and said, "I told you that trap spelled danger for all of us and now that is the end of the goat."

The king's son died. The king asked his servants to kill the bull to feed the people who had come for the son's funeral. The mouse stood there and said to itself, "I told everyone that trap spelled danger, and everyone said the trap was for me. I did my part in warning the community about the danger. Even an "idiot" has wisdom and a place in community. We can't do without each the other, small or big."

In indigenous contexts, each individual owes their survival and well-being to the community. The Africans of Zimbabwe believe that we were not created to be alone, neither in this world, nor in the world to come. When we ignore other's problems, those problems may later turn to become ours. Community problems are not to be ignored, since what affects other humans, in turn, affects us.

Knowing the Past Helps Us Know the Truth

In the West, we have a poem coming out of World War II. It shares the true story of Pastor Niemoeller during the Second World War. His experience of Hitler and the Nazis might be a good reminder to Westerners, as well to help all of us learn about the essence of life in community. What we learn from this holocaust poem is that we are a global community, not islands. Dr. Franklin H. Littell, a Methodist minister, college professor, Holocaust expert, scholar, and world citizen, contributed and wrote commentary on Martin Niemoeller, a respected Protestant leader in Germany and an opponent of Hitler during the Nazis regime. Littell writes about how Martin Niemoeller's poem has been misused and misquoted; however, he says the following is the original order and way the powerful writing first appeared:

> First they came for the communists, and I did not speak out–
> because I was not a communist;
> Then they came for the socialists, and I did not speak out—
> because I was not a socialist;
> Then they came for the trade unionists, and I did not speak
> out—because I was not a trade unionist;
> Then they came for the Jews, and I did not speak out—
> because I was not a Jew;
> Then they came for me—and there was no one left to speak
> out for me.[8]

The lines in this poem ring true in our contemporary world in how we need each other in working against the evils and suffering humanity is experiencing everywhere. We usually read or hear about tragedies

8. Littell, "First They Came for the Jews."

and ignore them thinking, "it is far away; it will not affect me." The essence of life in the global village today is not about distance, nationality, or race, but more about the survival of humanity. Sometimes the suffering may not be immediate, but will effect generations to come, just as memories of slavery and the holocaust still affect us today.

One of the best illustrations for building on the idea of the global village is in 1 Corinthians where the Apostle Paul writes about how there is one body, but many members to it.

> Indeed, the body does not consist of one member but of many. If the foot would say, "Because I am not a hand, I do not belong to the body," that would not make it any less a part of the body. . . . The eye cannot say to the hand "I have no need of you," nor again the head to the feet, I have no need of you. On the contrary, the members of the body that seem to be weaker are indispensable . . . But God has so arranged the body, giving the greater honor to the inferior member, that there may be no dissension within the body, but the members may have the same care for one another. If one member suffers, all suffer together with it, if one member is honored, all rejoice together with it. (1 Cor 12:13–26)

It is essential that the global community look at the problems around the world as ones that are right in their backyard. Just as in the passage above by the Apostle Paul says, most Africans believe that "the evil which befalls my neighbor befalls me." It is only a foolish neighbor who watches and is amused to see a neighbor struggle with life, for tomorrow greater evil will befall the one who watches. Thus I cannot tell the story of my life without including that of my neighbor. The mere fact that we are neighbors forces our stories to interweave or intertwine. Sooner or later, my neighbor's problems will have an effect on me, even though initially they do not appear to have such an effect.

Revillaging: A Blending of the Past and the Present

Many Shona Christians identify with the story of the struggle of the children of Israel coming out of Egypt to Canaan. From the time God appeared to Moses, and throughout their wilderness journey, the Israelites were to know that God was the God of Abraham, Isaac, and Jacob, and therefore God was to be remembered from generation to generation (Exod 3:15). The children of Israel were to recite these stories in their gatherings as a reminder that the God who delivered their forefathers was still the God who cared for them. As has been argued in earlier chapters, the culture and worldview of the Shona context today have been highly influenced by the Western culture and Westernized Christianity. The Bible has become central to the everyday lives of Shona Christians and, therefore, needs to be integrated into their modern-day, unfolding story. In addition, they need to remember, as well as to reclaim, some of the traditional village values.

Revillaging is the idea of reclaiming the core values of traditional Africa as explored in previous chapters. In traditional Africa, the village provided the cultural and religious foundations for the African. It was in the village that one got his or her psychological, mental, physical, and spiritual support, upbringing, and identity.

The advent of colonization and the continued influence of Westernization and capitalism have shaken the foundations of the African village today. At times, indigenous people seem to be persons running away from themselves, with a no known end goal. Traditionally a village was composed of the people (the living or those usually related through blood or marriage), the presence of the "living dead" or the "cloud of witness," the stories told of the past and present, the environment (nature, animals, rivers), communal mores and ethics, and a sense of belonging both spiritually and physically to the community.

Today many communities are made up of people who simply live next door to one anther because they happen to build or buy the home next door, especially in the urban areas. In many cases, people are not related by blood and may even not know much about one another. There is a need to reestablish a sense of the "village," with a specific focus on the orphans and widows in modern-day indigenous contexts, especially in the rural areas. The model I am proposing is that of revillaging—with the church providing the best place to attempt these revillaging efforts. This model is not just a theory to be tested but a model that is in existence in a few communities and that has already found success in some with which I have been involved. The model will be expounded upon in the next chapter under the section on holistic approaches to narrative pastoral counseling. For now, let me say that the reason for using the "church," or the local church, in this process is that the church is a group of people with a particular common "story" and belief system. Tying them together is Christ, who forms the foundation for revillaging. The definition of "revillaging" used in this chapter is borrowed from an unpublished paper that Ed Wimbelry and I presented in Cameroon.

> Re-villaging refers to the attempt . . . to re-establish selective village functions such as symbolizing, support/maintenance, ritualizing, and mentoring . . . a) Symbolizing function is the organizing of the life of the village around a particular story and sub-stories that provide an overarching system that gives meaning to every aspect of life; b) Support/maintenance function provides cross-generational relational ties for people that help them maintain emotional, physical, and spiritual well being in the face of life transitions and difficulty; c) Mentoring function refers to providing the next generation opportunities to be integrated into the community's meaning system through their internalization of attitudes, scenes, roles, and story plots; d) Ritualizing function provides repetitive patterns for re-enforcing symbolizing, support/maintenance, and mentoring functions.[9]

The African community is a storytelling community. Through story, identities are formed and healing is achieved. Africans believe that healing cannot be achieved until personal stories of both joy and suffering are told and heard. It is in the stories that people are able to discern were God is at work in their daily lives.

Revillaging Orphaned Children through the Church

Narrative counseling theory proposes that we live the story of our lives, and the story that we live is socially constructed. The stories that we live out are based out of the communities in which we find ourselves embedded. It was natural in traditional Africa that the elders would sit around the fire in the evenings and verbally pass on family, community, and clan stories. Individuals also shared their stories of pain, hope, and joy in the same setting. This was the palaver, where people were given the opportunity to retell personal, family, and even religious stories of how God was active in the community. (In the next chapter, I will go into further details about the palaver system and how it can be reclaimed in our modern-day indigenous contexts.) In this setting, as stated above, village and personal life were organized "around a particular story and

9. Wimberly and Mucherera, "Re-Villaging, Crisis Theory, and the African Context."

sub-stories that provided an overarching system giving meaning to every aspect of life."[10] The palaver was that place where people came to share their stories of joy and successes, pain or shame; and in the end, these stories evolved into stories of hope with the support and input of other family members or villagers.

It is my conviction that the church can provide that function again today. Many of the orphans in the rural areas turn to the church for help and support. The church can re-create the palaver for these children, can provide them with a place where they can come and share their personal stories of struggle. At the church palaver, they can hear others' personal struggles and victories, biblical stories, folktales, and community stories that will inspire hope. It is usually the case that when one shares one's struggles with other humans and then senses compassion from them, the burden, though not totally lifted, becomes lighter.

The church community is cross-generational by nature, as the palaver was. Traditionally the village used to provide (through the elders, aunts, uncles, grandfathers and grandmothers) emotional, spiritual, and mental development for the younger generations. In essence, the village provided a place for life transitions. In these days of HIV/AIDS, the church can once again rely on the surviving elders in the village or in the cities to provide direction for these orphans. The largest generation gap in existence today is between orphans (up to eighteen years old) and those elders who are sixty-plus years old. Many of those between the ages of nineteen and fifty-five years of age have died or are living with HIV/AIDS.

Forging these types of relationships will help the younger generations find the support they need. In addition, the elders involved in these processes will also benefit from these relationships, for in mentoring these youngsters they will find meaning and something to look forward to every day. One of the goals is for the younger generations to carry and then pass along the community's success stories. In this scenario, the elders involved in this cross-generational relationship also help the young orphans emotionally and spiritually, especially in the face of difficult life transitions. As will be elaborated in the next chapter, these mentors will get support from the church to help provide for the children's physical needs. I am involved with such projects that

10. Ibid.

are supporting orphans with basics such as food, clothing, and even school fees. Once every week mentors visit the children to make sure their physical needs are provided for. In other words, there is also a social service approach to this mentoring program. Mentoring must be holistic, making sure the physical, emotional, and spiritual needs of the children are made available. I will address the need for the establishment of children's orphan funds or children's trust funds in these communities as a way to help orphaned children with their needs.

The lack of mentors in communities is not just an African problem; but common knowledge is that many countries worldwide lack mentors for the younger generation. In a mentoring relationship, the mentor teaches by action. Based on church-type mentoring relationships, sometimes the mentor can disclose struggles and vulnerabilities through testimonies in prayer or section meetings. The mentor is put in the public eye of the mentee so that the mentor can safely and publicly express pain, suffering, and joy in the presence of the mentee. This creates a relationship where the two are not just emotionally supporting each other but become spiritual partners while being accountable to each other by regularly praying with and for each other. It is very possible for one mentor to have more than one mentee. As stated above, the mentor becomes one who provides the next generation with means to be integrated into the community through communicating the attitudes and roles, and biblical, communal and personal story plots forming his or her own story.

Everyone knows that for one to form behavior patterns, there has to be some repetitive patterns—rituals. Rituals help reinforce positive desired outcomes. In this model, one of the rituals is attending the church palaver or prayer meetings. It must be a daily ritual for the mentor to pray for the mentee privately and publicly by name at these church palavers or prayer meetings, or in worship services. When it becomes second nature for the mentor to provide this kind of support, the mentoring relationship becomes natural.

Some of the revillaging issues that will be addressed in further detail in the next chapter are: self-care in the age of HIV/AIDS and skills training. Other struggles worthy of our attention are issues of "youth identity confusion," being caught between cultures (referred to earlier as *masalala*, or the salad generation—a generation with no "home" culturally). These issues are addressed in more detail in my other work.[11]

But for now it is enough to say that young men and women, through these palavers, have to be mentored to respect themselves as respect pertains to sexual relations. In this age of the HIV/AIDS pandemic, they need to be mentored to practice abstinence and to be reminded that self-worth is not based on how many people with whom you have intercourse. It is good training to remind them that what they may have observed or picked up through the media about sexual relations is based on Hollywood and not reality. These youths need some structure, and mentors who are open to listening to their survival stories and perspectives. Not only do they need mentors; they also need trained "care mothers" or older women who are willing to be surrogate mothers. It is common for most people around the world to have someone they look up to for guidance or as a role model (much of this model will be fleshed out in the next chapter under the section on working with youth in the age of the HIV/AIDS pandemic).

The above revillaging efforts are between the orphaned youth and older adults. However, revillaging is not limited to young orphans. It is needed for other groups as well, such as women and men. Using the same idea of the church palaver or prayer meetings, the same type of support could be afforded to others, especially to widows. In this book, I have chosen to focus on the plight of women (widows) and children (orphans), because these are the groups for which I am most concerned. There are also some cultural issues with women and girls (addressed in earlier chapters) that I am interested in addressing through these church palavers. I simply cannot address all of the issues involved in the African context in this one book. Therefore, I have chosen to focus on widows and orphans, and perhaps someday will write another manuscript addressing other populations.

Revillaging and the Widow

As stated above, my not taking up problems facing men does not mean that men do not have issues they need to confront. In the same palaver setting, some of the men's issues as well as those of widows could be addressed. The issues that widows usually deal with are those of

11. Mucherera, *Pastoral Care from a Third World Perspective*.

inheritance, loss of extended family support, and HIV/AIDS. There are situations where the widow may discover she is HIV positive but still carries the burden of supporting her children. Without specifically focusing on men's issues, their issues will be touched upon as the situation of the widows is sorted out. The issue of inheritance, with its male counterissues, puts strains on family relations, thereby resulting in the widow's losing vital extended family support.

Using some of the revillaging methods above, the widow can find a place of solace at "church palavers," where she can share her emotional and physical burdens. The main function of these activities is to form a place where the widow can come, pray, and share her daily struggles with a group of other widows with whom she can identify. This is the palaver, an informal group where people come together to hear and heal each other's pain.

This type of setting is formed out of the indigenous context's understanding that "one can never heal alone." Healing is both an individual and a communal activity. Life is connected, such that even the medicine person cannot heal him- or herself, but will have to go to another medicine person for healing. Usually it is believed that one cannot heal emotional or spiritual wounds alone since these hurts occur within the context of community or relationships.

Life is a web—every thread in the web contributes to the strength or beauty of the web. Each and every day of our lives we spin a thread or create a piece of the web that adds to our story and thereby adds to the community story. The widows, who come together to retell their stories, are creating a web that is stronger. In the next chapter, I will also share specific scenarios and stories I have encountered in working with some of the widows, for through story is often how we learn best.

Reauthoring: Hope through the "Barrel" of the Pen

The story of the African people needs to be moved from a footnote to the main text. The African community can no longer afford to sit, wallowing in our tears. It is important to understand the past, but it does not help one to continue to dwell on the past and not find new ways to forge into the future. As has commonly been said, history repeats itself. Indigenous people have learned that "life is a cycle of both good and bad." They have learned that there are days of plenty and days of want.

There are days to build and days to plunder or be plundered. Before colonialism, there were intertribal wars, famines, diseases, and other forms of suffering. However, all these sufferings did not wipe out the people of the land, for there was always a remnant to give hope to the next generation.

Hope is the only key to survival. A people without hope will easily perish. The stories, cultures, and traditions of indigenous people were distorted and subjugated by the early Western writers and are still being marginalized and dominated even today. And in Christian theological circles as well, voices of indigenous people remain marginalized, even in their own contexts. One has just to visit an educational institution such as a seminary in an indigenous context to see what books are being used to teach and train theological students and pastors. As Michael White, an Australian narrative therapist, asserts: human beings are interpretive beings in seeking meaning.[12] Much of what has been written about indigenous people (even today) is an interpretation of the indigenous people's stories by Westerners through Western lenses. One's interpretation of events is based on prior experiences.

Today indigenous people are in the process of rewriting communal or faith narratives that have been marginalized, or perceived and labeled as backwards and primitive. One of the tasks of the contemporary indigenous person is the process of "normalizing" that which had been labeled "abnormal" from his or her historical past, creating gaps in the narratives of today's contemporary indigenous context. It is the duty and undertaking of those who can publish, and who are given the platform, to free indigenous people from dominant Western narratives, and yet at the same time without indiscriminately throwing away some of the stories (biblical and others) that have become part of the story of today's indigenous peoples. What is important is to be able to weave together these hopeful scriptural stories with personal stories to form a new paradigm—a new and hopeful story. Part of the work of this reauthoring process is to help liberate many of the indigenous people's minds from the inferiority complex created by the West.

Effectiveness in any environment demands that one be familiar with the cultural context in which one finds oneself working. The narrative-therapy or narrative-counseling approach rightly acknowledges

---

12. White and Epson, *Narrative Means to Therapeutic Ends,* 2ff.

the influence of the social construction of realities on individuals and their communities. Jill Freedman and Gene Combs see the social construction of realities as "the way in which every person's social, interpersonal reality has been constructed through interaction with other human beings and human institutions and to focus on the influence of social realities on the meaning of people's lives." [13]

Humans create cultures, and in turn their cultural environment shapes who humans become. As much as humans are born with minds, the societies that they are born into, or the people they belong to, help construct their realities and worldviews. In other words, humans are shaped by their relationships in their communities of embeddedness. Freedman and Combs further say:

> The beliefs, values, institutions, customs, labels, laws, divisions of labor, and the like that make up our social realities are constructed by the members of a culture as they interact with one another from generation to generation and day to day. That is, societies construct the "lenses" through which their members interpret the world. The realities that each of us takes for granted are the realities that our societies have surrounded us with since birth. These realities provide the beliefs, practices, words, and experiences from which we make up our lives, or as we would say in postmodernist jargon, "constitute our selves." [14]

The debate on the question of "how persons come to know what they know or claim to know" or, as it is called, "epistemology," is not new. This subject is relevant at this juncture as well. People in different cultures around the world learn differently, especially in those cultures that have been traditionally oral. People in these contexts come to know what they know through experience, observation, participation, symbols, and language. It is my belief that different cultures around the world may employ some of these modes of learning. Today in the indigenous context, we continue to struggle. The final thing we will need to shed is mental colonization, as the likes of Ngugi have written. [15] Until many indigenous people start believing in their core values and stop grabbing at everything Western, there will not be much progress in these communities. Indeed, there are Western values that need to be

13. Freedman and Combs, *Narrative Therapy*, 1.

14. Ibid., 16.

15. Ngugi wa Thiong'o, *Decolonising the Mind*.

accepted, but there are also traditional values that need to be reclaimed, and this all needs to be written down for the next generation to pass on. It is the task of intellectual workers and modern-day indigenous writers to free our people by reauthoring and setting the history record right.

The intellectual worker is to be without bias, condemning abuse and misuse of power in the indigenous contexts as well. As stated earlier, it does not get us anywhere to blame all the problems experienced by indigenous peoples solely on colonization. The unjust postcolonial systems need to be confronted as well. As I write, Zimbabwe is going through turmoil. Violence escalated soon after the March 29, 2008, elections and continues, with many of the members of the opposition parties being killed or arrested. Talks between the government and the opposition parties have not resulted in a peaceful resolution. The economic situation is worse than in any other country under the sun. The governor of the Reserve Bank of Zimbabwe (RBZ) introduced a 100-billion Zimbabwean dollar note on July 18, 2008, but government officials seem to be blind to these bad economic realities. The current regime has been in power for twenty-eight years, and it is time for a change. The great signpost of hope for the people of Zimbabwe would be for these leaders to allow for change to take its own course. By the time this book is published, I hope we will be talking about a new Zimbabwe—a country that used to be the breadbasket of southern central Africa. The signs of hope are being experienced through the pressure that the international community is placing upon the present regime to concede power.

I have argued that some of the theological signposts of hope in indigenous contexts such as Zimbabwe are religion, revillaging, and reauthoring. Even in the face of death, the poor and the HIV/AIDS infected and affected have their hope set on God. In addition, their hope is also set on the understanding that as humans we are all connected; we are in it together. In creating mentoring relationships, we are giving hope to the younger generation and to future generations. Finally, it is the task of intellectual workers to set the record straight through the "barrel of the pen," in decolonizing our minds. In addition, it is the job of intellectual workers to challenge corrupt and oppressive postcolonial governments who end creating economic crises due to being selfish and greedy.

The final chapter focuses on the palaver. The palaver will be further defined, and case stories will be presented to illustrate the method advocated in working with widows and orphans. The primary focus will be on ways to set up church palavers. Using the palaver setting, the chapter presents a holistic, narrative pastoral counseling approach in the age of the HIV/AIDS pandemic—a holistic approach that cares about the whole being: the mind, body, and spirit.

5

The Palaver and Beyond

*A Holistic, Narrative Pastoral Care
and Counseling Approach*

"Kuwanda huuya, mota yekumusana unoona anokutumbura."
("It is a blessing to be many; when you have an abscess
on your back where you cannot reach, you have others
to open and treat it.")

—Shona proverb

"Mauya, makadiniko?"
"Ndakasimba kana makasimbawo."

IN THIS COMMON exchange, the greeting translates: "Welcome," or "Hello. How are you?" The normal response is, "I am well, if you are well." The indication in these statements is that if those you meet or those who surround you are not well, you are not well either. If the person in the exchange of the greeting further responds by saying things are not well at his or her house because his or her children have had nothing to eat for the past few days, it now means that all is not well for these two who have just met. It now means that even if the person who had asked felt they were well, this person is no longer well until he or she has offered help or some social support to the unwell family. Health in indigenous or in the African Shona context is not just how a person is feeling; it is more than the absence of disease or illness: health and wellness cover the totality of life, such as economic, physical, mental, and spiritual concerns, including everything that a person may need in terms of social support to sustain life.

This applies to social isolation as well, for it is perceived as hazardous to one's health and wellness, and to life. This makes the application of counseling or therapy by one who is working in indigenous contexts very different from other applications in other contexts. In other words, there is more to holistic living that goes beyond one's mental health.

Relying on "talk therapy" or counseling alone with orphans and widows in indigenous contexts is cheap and will not always achieve desired goals. Counseling in the West tends to focus on the promotion of *autonomy* or the *independence* of a client, and counselors are perceived as "mental health professionals" who are not expected to go outside their "four walls" in service to the client. In this chapter, I put forth the argument that reclaiming the traditional understanding of palaver and adopting a holistic narrative counseling approach will benefit counselors whose goal is to work with orphans and widows in indigenous contexts.

First, I will attempt to show that the emphasis in counseling practices that focus on the intrapsychic alone will not always work in indigenous contexts; rather the work has to go beyond the mind to other human aspects. One of the key issues to intervention in these contexts, due to the HIV/AIDS pandemic and poverty, is to try to "save the body first," for a mind without a body is dead. Second, I will expound key components of a holistic approach suitable for these contexts. For the widows and orphans who might be HIV infected, the holistic approach might not offer them a *cure*, but will provide a place for *healing* emotionally, relationally, and spiritually. In indigenous contexts, because of the importance of community and family relations, it is necessary to balance finding a cure with providing a place for healing. Also, the palaver, its context and processes, and some of the concepts important to it will be defined. Finally, I will try to demonstrate how this approach can be applied, by using case scenarios from Zimbabwe. It must be said, however, this holistic narrative counseling approach is not limited to indigenous settings but is also applicable to other contexts where the services for widows and orphans are needed due to poverty and HIV/AIDS.

I am convinced that in our postmodern world today, despite all the deaths going on due to wars (especially in the Middle East), we have closed our eyes to the real WMDs ("weapons of mass destruction"): poverty and HIV/AIDS. We are treating these WMDs with kid gloves: If as humans we believed in true *interdependence*, most of the suffering in the world could easily be eliminated. I've always wondered how someone with billions of dollars in their bank accounts could easily go home and sleep comfortably at night after seeing the suffering of the homeless and the poor. Many of the "haves" have become blind and calloused to the suffering and plight of the "have-nots." This is not to put down the efforts of many "haves" who have set up foundations and put forth other efforts to help the poor and those affected by HIV/AIDS. Yet the stark reality is that the world seems to be operating on the principle of individualism: "each person for him- or herself, and God for us all." We forget that God created us for relationships and interdependence, especially with the poor of the poorest.

Balanced Interdependence versus Independence

Some Western ethical and moral guiding principles used in counseling in the indigenous context are autonomy, beneficence, and justice; yet autonomy is contrary to the practice of the palaver. One of the major goals of counseling, by Western standards, is to promote autonomy or independence: "Autonomy refers to the promotion of self-determination, or the freedom of clients to choose their direction. Respect for autonomy entails acknowledging the right of another to choose and act in accordance with his or her own wishes and requires the professional to behave in a way that enables this right."[1] In my experience working within indigenous contexts, this Western guiding principle is quite contrary even to the primary goal of counseling or therapy, which is to help a client maintain or achieve a balanced healthy interdependence with others. In the African context, one's life and stories unfold within the context of community, and it is therefore acknowledged that it is within community relations that health can be achieved. The Shona proverb cited above ("It is a blessing to be many; when you have an abscess on your back where you cannot reach, you have others to open and treat it") is a good indication of how counselors and therapists need to take healthy interdependence, versus independence or autonomy, into consideration. In an indigenous context, it is hard to perceive one as independent from

1. Corey, *Issues and Ethics*, 16ff.

family and community but rather is best to view healthy interdependence as the goal. In other words, the only independence that an orphaned child could easily achieve is through a healthy interdependence with and within the community in which the child is embedded. This applies not only to orphans but to all people of all ages.

How would anyone expect a twelve- or fourteen-year-old who has become a head of household (taking care of two or more siblings) to go through counseling that tries to help the child achieve autonomy or independence? As capable as these children are, "insight counseling" won't benefit them as much, since most of what is on the children's minds is survival, not only for the head child, but for the family as a whole. The primary goal with this type of child has more to do with basic needs such as food and clothing, therefore requiring the counselor to learn advocacy and social-service skills rather than simply to focus on the psychological and emotional health of the child. The argument does not put down the importance of mental health, but working with orphaned children demands more than mastering "talk therapy" or counseling skills, so as to be holistic.

Can you imagine a counselor, who has had a full breakfast or lunch, spending fifty minutes counseling a child who looks worn out and hasn't had a meal in three days? These are some of the conditions in indigenous contexts; counselors have to be trained to be aware of and to intervene in these settings. Such competence reaches beyond understanding the basic attending, listening, and interviewing skills.

God has always been concerned about the welfare of orphan and the widow. In some of the earliest social and religious laws given to the children of Israel, they are warned about the wrath of God if they neglect orphans and the widows: "You shall not abuse any widow or orphan. If you do abuse them, when they cry; my wrath will burn, and I will kill you with the sword, and your wives shall become widows and your children orphans" (Exod 22:22–23). God's concern for widows and orphans still stands today, and those who wish to work with them, even in providing counseling, have to honor this command not out of fear of God's wrath, but out of compassion for widows and orphans.

The Body, Mind, and Spirit: A Holistic Approach

Counseling methods that can survive the test of time in indigenous contexts are the ones that are holistic in nature. These types of counseling approach have to take into consideration the totality of the human being that is body, mind, and spirit. At times the counselors may have to work as a team with those outside of their profession in order to help the child. Circumstances may require the counselor to go and see where the orphan lives and sleeps, and what he or she eats, in order to fully understand the child's predicament. When working with orphans, the passage from the New Testament letter of James rings true:

> What good is it, my brothers and sisters, if you have faith but do not have works? Can faith save you? If a brother or sister is naked and lacks daily food, and one of you says to them, "Go in peace; keep warm and eat your fill," and yet do not supply their bodily needs, what is the good of that? So faith by itself, if it has no works is dead. . . . For just the body without the spirit is dead, so faith without works is also dead. (Jas 2:14–26)

I fully concur with James's argument in the passage above. In a similar manner, effective counseling in indigenous contexts must explore the physical, mental (emotional and psychological), and spiritual needs of the person being served. A counselor may be very skilled in helping these children emotionally, but if the counselor has failed in connecting the child to finding the next meal, that counselor has only done half the work. Indigenous contexts call for counselors to "get off the couch or chair" and into the streets. This is a maverick strategy compared with the status quo in counseling methods and approaches. The tendency of many approaches developed in the Western world to focus mainly on the psychological or mental well-being of persons falls short.

Being healthy in the indigenous contexts is not limited to the "mind" but includes matters of faith/spirituality and the body as well. It is therefore essential that a holistic, narrative pastoral counseling approach be applied in working with orphans, assessing and servicing the three basic areas of human need: the body, mind, and spirit.

The body is serviced by making sure the counselor understands the physical needs of the child or at least connecting the child with someone who can help service those needs. In serving the mind, the counselor's priority is making sure the emotional and psychological needs of the child are attended. Besides talking one-on-one with the child, the counselor must make sure the child is connected to a palaver setting where the child can share struggles with others. The spiritual aspect is usually one of the areas in counseling that is neglected but cannot be ignored in these contexts. As stated earlier, in most indigenous contexts it is hard for people to separate religion and culture. Usually, religion is a way of life. It is, therefore, important that these children are helped to understand God in their predicaments—in the losses of their parents and the resultant anger and grief they may experience. Again, neglecting any of these areas falls short of a holistic counseling approach and will not fully service the child. The point is, humans are not just physical creatures; neither are they only emotional; nor are they just spiritual beings. Rather, human beings are essentially all three of these aspects of their being, equally.

The Body: Without One, One is as Good as Dead

Convinced that a holistic approach in caring for orphans was what was needed to address their physical needs, and knowing the predicament of many of the orphans in Zimbabwe in 1997, I led a mission trip of twenty-three people from St. Luke's United Methodist Church of Highlands Ranch, Colorado, to Chitimbe, in Murewa.[2] We purchased a grinding mill and helped construct the building to house the mill. The construction work was done together with the locals. It was quite a partnership, which endeavored to help the orphans in the community. Uzumba Orphan Trust became a model for many communities on how to support orphans in their environment without moving them to orphanages. The main goal was to establish community-based care for the orphans. When we departed from Zimbabwe, we left the Uzumba community with a grinding mill to support over five hundred orphaned children. Over US $2,000 were also left as the start-up amount for diesel fuel and a repair fund for the mill. With the establishment of the grinding mill, the Uzumba Orphan Trust project attracted the attention of UNICEF, Southern African AIDS Trust (SAT), the General Board of Global ministries[3] and many other NGOs, as a model program to support children orphaned by HIV/AIDS. The vision from this project grew and spread around the whole country of Zimbabwe. When the orphan trust was established, some of the goals were

2. Gilbert, "Zimbabwe: How Can We Help Now?"

3. Butler, "It Really Does Take a Village."

To mobilize resources for sustainability through the introduction of projects like grinding mills, poultry, piggery, etc.; assist orphans spiritually, morally, materially, and train them in survival skills so as to be self-reliant; to economically empower the women-volunteer care givers through training and assisting them in starting their own income generating projects like tie and dye; to reduce the menace of HIV/AIDS through workshops and education, and encouraging behavioral change.[4]

A local committee along with the help of many volunteers runs these types of projects. People in the rural areas still take their grain there to be ground, and they pay the miller for the grinding. The profit from the milling is what is used to support the orphans in the local area. In addition, caregivers are given training in assessing the physical needs of the orphans, such as food, clothing, living environment, and health. If the caregivers find that a child under their care is ill but has not gone to the clinic or hospital, it is the job of the caregivers to assist in getting that child the help needed.

The common saying that goes, "if you give a person a fish, you feed him or her for a day, but if you teach a person to fish, you have fed him or her for life," is a driving force behind such projects. In addition, the grinding mill is also used to grind feed for the raising of poultry and pigs. The goal in this whole project is to feed, as well as to give some basic skills to, local orphans in order that they might be self-sufficient or at least able to support their own physical needs. Some of the older children are involved in the raising of chickens, in growing vegetable gardens, and in other similar projects. The caregivers also make sure that the children are safe, and that they don't live in fear of abuse. It is my conviction that if holistic pastoral care and counseling are to be beneficial in these contexts, one must pay close attention to practical ways of supporting the orphans, aiding them in ways to become self-sustaining in their physical needs.

After moving to Kentucky in 1999 to take a teaching position at Asbury Seminary, I became co-pastor of Mt. Zion United Methodist Church near Shakertown. I served with the Rev. Dr. Jim Thobaben, a professor of Christian ethics at Asbury Seminary. Dr. Thobaben and I decided to give the stipend that the church was offering us to the church's mission budget—more specifically towards supporting

4. Musodza and Chitiyo, "Uzumba Orphan Trust," 2.

orphans in Zimbabwe. This challenged the laypeople, and they soon took it upon themselves to increase their giving. When on sabbatical in 2003, I went to Zimbabwe to do research, and during that time established two projects to support orphans in their own contexts (rather than moving them to orphanages) at Gwese and Chibuwe. Similar to the project described above, we bought a grinding mill for each of the communities. Between 2004 and 2006, four more grinding mills were added—one at Fairfield Orphanage (Old Mutare Mission Hospital), another at Murombedzi Growth Point, one at Bindura United Methodist Church, and the last one at Mhakwe Primary School in the Mutambara area. These projects were birthed out of Mt. Zion's vision of supporting the orphans. Today when all the six (6) grinding mills are running, they are supporting three thousand orphaned children per day. These projects aid the orphans with school fees, uniforms, food, and any other necessary provisions for physical needs—*taking care of the body.*

Feeding Programs

In order not to miss some of the children, especially the ones that are still very young, there are now feeding programs established, usually at a central location such as a school or a church. "Care-mothers" in these locations prepare and feed porridge to the children every morning. The porridge is made from cornmeal (ground maize), with peanut butter or other nutrients added to it. In some of these communities, the cornmeal comes from the community grinding-mill projects. Some of the care-mothers travel six miles one way every morning to prepare the porridge for the children. The children are fed during the morning school break if it is during school days, or around midmorning during school holidays.

These feeding programs are now found in many parts of Zimbabwe today, supported by organizations such as the United States Agency for International Development (USAID), World Vision International, and others.[5] The drive behind all of this is to save and support the physical wellness of these children, and to literally "save the body first." Many of the local United Methodist churches in Zimbabwe are behind the start-up of the feeding programs, especially in the rural areas. They start the programs and then seek assistance from other global partners

5. Muchapera, "World Vision Launches Urban School Feeding Program."

as the programs continue.[6] It is also common knowledge that a child's performance in school is hindered by a lack of good nutrition. Again, the focus is to take care of the physical needs of the children in trying to achieve this holistic pastoral counseling approach to care.

One of the perspectives that we as counselors need to take is based on Jesus Christ's earthly ministry. The Scriptures and the ministry of Jesus Christ are a good indication of how we need care especially for those who are less fortunate. The Bible, in general, is full of passages where prophets warn communities and individuals about the wrath of God for those who neglect the orphan and the widow (Isa 10:1–3; Jer 7:5–7, 22:2–5; Zech 7:9–11; Mal 3:5). In addition, several Old Testament and New Testament Scripture passages address the issues of taking care of the widows and orphans (Jas 1:27; 1 Tim 5:9–16; Deut 10:17–18; Isa 1:17). The care of and ministry to widows and orphans is not new but something that has always been a part of the Judeo-Christian heritage.

Jesus's Ministry as Our Example

Through his ministry, Jesus showed that his concern for people was not limited to spiritual or emotional needs but concerned the whole person. One of the first things Jesus does in the temple early in his ministry is to indicate his identity and mission, quoting a passage from the prophet Isaiah as the fulfillment of who he is and of what he is to do.

> The spirit of the Lord is upon me, because he has anointed me to bring good news to the poor. He has sent me to proclaim release to the captives and recovery of sight to the blind, to let the oppressed go free, to proclaim the year of the Lord's favor. (Luke 4:18–19)

Jesus's ministry was not only focused on spiritual needs but also on physical aspects of people's lives. In chapters 6 and 8 in the Gospel of Mark, Jesus is described as having compassion for the crowds that had been with him for three days without anything to eat. He doesn't want to send them away hungry, for their homes are too far away. On these two occasions, Jesus shows that he cares about people's physical well-being. In fact, he performs a miracle that multiplies two fish and a few loaves of bread that are available in order to feed five thousand and

---

6. Abiot Moyo, "Mission Team Returns from Zimbabwe."

four thousand people respectively (Mark 6:30–44, 8:1–9). His healing miracles also show that Jesus is concerned about both the physical as well as the spiritual well-being of people.

In one instance, while talking to his disciples and those gathered, Jesus tells the parable quoted below, about how the nations will be judged because of the neglect of the poor and of those needing support. The point here is not how the counselor will be judged at the end of the age, but rather the importance of being holistic in our practice.

> Then the king will say to those at his right hand, "Come, you that are blessed by my father, inherit the kingdom prepared for you from the foundation of the world; for I was hungry and you gave me food, I was thirsty and you gave me something to drink, I was a stranger and you welcomed me, I was naked and you gave me clothing, I was sick and you took care of me, I was in prison and you visited me." . . . Then he will say to those at the left hand, "You that are accursed, depart from me . . . , for I was hungry and you gave me no food, I was thirsty and you gave me nothing to drink, I was a stranger and you did not welcome me, naked and you did not give me clothing." (Matt 25:31–44)

The above passage is one of those where Jesus shows that he views his ministry as one that offered people more than just spiritual salvation, and rather as concerned about the totality of human beings. It is my conviction that one of the primary areas in serving the orphans and the widows is making sure their physical needs are provided for.

In summary, one of the guiding principles in indigenous narrative pastoral counseling is to save the body first, without which one can do little, if anything, other than bury the body. Having found ways to meet the basic needs of the orphans, it is then important to work with them psychologically, mentally, emotionally, and spiritually. This work can take place at palavers done in local homes, churches, or schools. Below I describe the general aspects of the palaver, such as its concepts, the environment, and the processes.

A Palaver: In Service to the Mind and Soul

What is a palaver? There are different types of palaver, depending on the issue and who is involved; however, the goal of any palaver is the same—to resolve a problem, crisis, or conflict and to make other

time for educational purposes or just simply for fellowship. At one level, with the coming of Westernization, the modern Western court systems replaced the tribal or community palavers that had formed to make decisions. Other kinds of palavers are those offered by a clan or family. Today what is still common is the family palaver. The meeting can be open or closed, depending on the crisis or problem. Robert G. Armstrong translates the word *palaver* into a more recognizable phrase, "the public meeting." He says, "We could only mean by such a concept 'any gathering of an organized group in a formal manner'. . . [T]he palaver also takes place through persons, usually [elders] who are close to both group and leader, or it can be a person who has a particular problem to settle . . . This form of palaver is quite common . . . and helps solve concrete problems arising in families, such as divorce, marriage, family disputes, etc."[7] In other words, a palaver was and is one of the key traditional African methods for providing individuals and community a context for emotional processing and healing.

I remember growing up in the rural areas of Zimbabwe in the 1970s enjoying the evening (*kudare*) palavers as a child. The palaver was the place where I sat in a circle with the elders around the fire. The girls would be in the house or kitchen with the older women around the fire as well. The elders would tell us both entertaining and moral stories. They gave us, the children, riddles to solve, and it was a place where one was educated about the culture. There were two types of palaver—one for education or fellowship and the other to resolve family or community problems. Most of my education about Shona culture, its values, and how to be a gentleman came from the palaver. I remember moments when people shared their struggles and the pains of the day. The elders would ask questions about these daily problems, share their insights through a riddle or folktale, and those around the fire offered words of wisdom or encouragement. This is one of the types of palaver being lost in these indigenous contexts, which I want to focus on in this book. This type of the palaver needs to be reclaimed for the sake and service of the orphaned children.

A counseling approach that uses story to resolve problems is natural for most people who grow up in indigenous contexts; hence the narrative approach is commonly used at the palaver. In this chapter,

---

7. Armstrong, *Socio-political Aspects of the Palaver*, 16, 29.

concepts that are common to Narrative Counseling in general are used; however, these same concepts may be used differently in the African or Zimbabwean contexts.

Similar to the descriptions given above, in a traditional palaver, people usually sit in a circle, and usually around a fire, or under a tree. Community palavers usually take place in the afternoon, while family palavers are in the evening or at night. This chapter will focus on a setting similar to an evening family palaver in working with the community orphans.

The Modern-Day Palaver

This modern-day palaver, also referred to as the church palaver, is no longer solely focused on resolving emotional problems or simply taking care of the mind. It is also a place for children to get spiritual support, and where they can come to fellowship and pray. The palaver meetings with the children are held weekly at a local church, school, or in the home of one of the elders. Initially, all present meet in a large group where they pray and worship together. After the worship and prayer time, the children are divided along gender lines, with the girls meeting with the elder women and the boys with the men. In Zimbabwe, these types of palavers would take place at events similar to Wednesday or Sunday evening prayer meetings. Depending on the number of people participating, the girls and boys would be divided into smaller groups of about ten to twelve members, or they would all remain in one group, similar to group counseling.

The leader or community elder facilitating each of the small palaver groups opens the meetings and assures the gathered that everyone is given voice, a chance to share and contribute, or the opportunity to ask questions. In narrative counseling, those seated in the circle are considered "outsider-witnesses." Morgan defines outsider-witnesses as two or more audience members known or unknown to the counselee, or people agreed upon by the counselor and the counselee, who may offer relevant experience.[8] The difference between the African palaver and a North American narrative counseling session] is that as part of the palaver] everyone who is part of the circle is considered an outsider-witness, is fully a member of, and can contribute to the conversations

---

8. Morgan, *What is Narrative Therapy*, 121.

at the palaver. In other words, the counselee does not have much voice over who sits at the palaver unless this is a closed palaver. Most who participate in family or community palavers are close relatives or known community members. These people come not to disrupt or scorn the person; rather their goal is to help fight the problem at hand.

After people are settled and have shared formal greetings, the elder or facilitator opens the meeting by telling those at the palaver that here they have a safe place to share, and then asks if there are any joys or concerns. The facilitator can ask a general question, such as, "What joys or problems do we have to share today?" If there is a specific problem (shared by someone at the palaver) already known to the facilitator, the facilitator may open the meeting by saying, "There is a problem or crisis being experienced by one or more people in the circle that 'we' have to help resolve." The use of "we" gives ownership to all those gathered at the palaver to tackle the problem as if it were their own. For the people who are experiencing the problem, hearing "we" helps them to hear that the problem or crisis is no longer just their "burden to carry" but is shared by those in the circle.

The facilitator/elder may also ask the first open-ended question to the person with the crisis or problem: "What problem, crisis or narrative brings you to the palaver assembly today?" The emphasis is on the problem rather than the person. The goal here is to try to create an environment for all gathered to view the "problem as the problem," not the person. The facilitator/elder's opening question is usually an *externalizing* one. White and Denborough say:

> Externalizing conversations are conversations that create space for the people to see themselves as separate from the problems that are affecting their lives. Once the problem is seen as separate from the identity of a person or from the identity of a significant relationship, the person is in a position to take new action.[9]

Many of the indigenous settings, especially in the African context, continue to use the oral tradition and storytelling in problem solving. One of the best examples of the externalizing processes at the palaver is when animal folktales (animals as players) are used in trying to come up with solutions, rather than using specific people's stories. When stories are told using animals or other symbols as characters, or when proverbs

---

9. White and Denborough, *Introducing Narrative Therapy,* 219.

are used, it becomes much easier for the person to talk about a problem as if it were outside of oneself. It gives the person an opportunity to attack the problem directly, without feeling attacked. In addition, metaphors are also used to describe feelings that one has lost the words for expression. Metaphors have a way of giving voice and expression to that which can be emotionally overwhelming. In most indigenous contexts, people still use proverbs, idioms, or sayings as an easier way to narrate their crisis or problem.

The elder facilitating the discussion makes sure that the conversations continue to be, or remain externalized. One of the key aspects is to have the persons or person narrating the problem comes up with a specific name for the problem. "*Naming the problem* is negotiating a definition of the problem that fits with the meaning and experience of the person whose life the problem is affecting."[10] Naming gives one some sense of power and/or charge over "the thing or problem" affecting him/her. It gives the one naming a sense of mental "jurisdiction," and of being able to put into words that which has been overwhelming to an extent that one has lost words to describe.

After having named the problem, the conversation may take the direction of understanding how this "issue, crisis, problem or thing" might be affecting the individual, and/or his/her relationships. Some of the general questions asked are: What happened or what is your story? What is happening now in your life? What do you need from us now as a community or as individuals? What do you wish for the future? What gives you hope? Are there instance in your life where you have experienced God's hand, and if so, in what way? What have you been able to discern as God's purpose for your life?

The conversations continue to move from what Morgan describes as a "thin" to a "rich and thick description." A thin description is when one's story does not allow for "life's complexities and contradictions," while in a rich and thick description "an alternative story that can be richly described" emerges.[11] In this context, the idea is to provide those at the palaver a thicker description of what might have taken place or is taking place in the person's life. The questions raised trace the history of the problem, how the problem started, and how it has affected the

---

10. Morgan, *What Is Narrative Therapy?* 44, italics added.

11. Ibid., 13–14.

person. Other important questions include when the problem is normally present, with whom and under what circumstances. There is the idea of "exceptions"—that is, asking questions concerning the moments when the problem was not or is not present, or if there are moments when the problem is or was present but the person was still able to manage—"mastery experiences" or "unique outcomes." Part of this process is what is known as "deconstruction," meaning the dismantling of some of the false beliefs or of mystifying parts of the problem that one might have internalized.[12]

The goal of the process is *restorying*, meaning a process by which the person is helped to see his or her story in a different light.[13] Wimberly talks about the need to pay attention to themes that comes up in the narrations of life stories. He says these themes play a great part in the reauthoring or restorying processes. The reediting process involves (1) identifying the themes at work in the various mythologies in our lives, (2) mapping and charting the influences of these themes, (3) discerning where God's renewing influence is as we come to grips with these themes and their influences, and (4) making plans that will aid us in changing some of the themes.[14] The following are some examples of the questions one would ask during the restorying or reauthoring processes. (I have rephrased or reworded questions by Wimberly in the restorying processes.[15])

- What would it take for the problem to be different or to take a turn from the direction it is going?
- Are there people who need to be involved and/or rituals that may need to take place?
- How would the story about your problem look without the problem?
- What would be different about your relations when the problem is gone?

12. Ibid., 45ff.
13. Ibid., 15ff and 45ff.
14. Wimberly, *Recalling Our Own Stories*, 88.
15. Ibid., 88ff.

- What gives you hope in this new story about your relations, and who else outside of the palaver would love to listen to your new story?

- Are there any biblical stories with which or biblical characters with whom you identify? Are there some African folktales you identify with; if so, which ones, and how?

- Are there people God has used to help you to make it through this struggle, or who offer you a hopeful future?

- If you were to ask for one thing or miracle of God, what would that be?

Not all of these questions may be asked in each and every case, but people should ask those questions that are relevant to each circumstance. In the following section, I will illustrate how some of these questions can be used within a palaver with children.

Hear Their Stories: Children at the Palaver

> Rukariro, (boy, 14) is the oldest of three children who lost both parents to HIV/AIDS. He has become the head of the household, taking care of his two siblings Tatenda (girl, 12) and Tapiwa (boy, 10). Rukariro is finishing seventh grade and hoping to go to high school after sitting for the seventh-grade exam. However, the chances of his proceeding to high school are limited since he has become the head of the household. It is Rukariro's responsibility to make sure that Tatenda and Tapiwa stay in school, and that they are safe. Rukariro and the other siblings have a garden where they are raising vegetables. The two cattle they had were both slaughtered for food at their parents' funerals, leaving them to rely on neighbors for oxen to pull the plough in order for them to plow the fields. They have not been able to cultivate the fields in the last two years since their parents died. They are also raising some corn and other vegetables in the garden, but this is not enough to sustain them throughout the year.[16]

The case above is a common scenario of child-headed families. At a palaver, these children are encouraged to share their problems, usually with the eldest child doing much of the talking in the initial phases

---

16. This narrative is based on true scenarios happening with child-headed families.

if it is about the material needs they may have. However, in general, all the children are given an equal opportunity to share what is going on in their lives. One of the simple questions they would be asked is, what happened? Or, tell us your experiences during the time your parents found out about their illness, until the time of their deaths. This gives the children an opportunity to share about how they lost their parents. It gives them the chance to share how they had to take care of their dying parents, to express the fears they had of catching the disease, and to tell how they had to miss school to make sure their parents had the help they needed. In some cases, children will even share their wish to have been the ones who died first, knowing the struggles that still lie ahead of them. Children in such situations might also share how they were teased or even shunned by others who suspected them of having the disease. This, in some cases, creates a foreshortened sense of life, where children may become so focused on their own death rather than on the future. A sense of hopelessness grows within children in this situation if the children believe they won't live long because their parents are already dead.

Another important general question to ask is, what is happening currently in your life? This question helps children share any problematic issues they may be facing with having to do with family or neighbors. The children can share if there might be neighbors who may be showing tendencies of abuse toward them. This question also helps to assess the children's safety and to assure them that they will get the support they need. The above question may be followed by others such as, what do you need from us now? How can we be of help, or what would it take for the problem to take a different direction with our support? If there are practical needs that can be offered by those in the circle, then volunteers will give the children the support they need. Besides the fact that many of the children might have basic needs, some of them might actually say that all they need is to know or have the assurance that those in the circle will continue to be available and supportive. Others may also share that one of the most important things for them is to have this place to come and share with others, where they are accepted and don't feel judged as "those orphans." "Kutanga, tiri vanhu, handitingori nherera chete" translates as, "We are people first; we are not 'just' those orphans." Children need to see the palaver as a safe place where they are treated with dignity and respect.

It is important to understand that in the midst of all the struggles orphans have, most of them are given hope through such groups. Another question to help them explore and express hope is, what gives you hope for the future, and has God used anyone to foster that hope? An answer I have heard in many instances is, "It is people like you, in this circle, who don't judge us based on our circumstances, who keep our lives going—people who genuinely treat us with unconditional love and not like the scum or rubbish of the society—that is what gives us hope. There is nothing so great as being visible and being seen as created in the image of God. Even though we lost our blood father and mother to death by HIV/AIDS, you the elders, and everyone else concerned, have become our mothers and fathers. Above all, we have our greatest hope in God the Father, who created us—the Father who cares for us all."

Sometimes the children might not have had the chance to openly grieve because they were so involved with the death of their parents and the burial arrangements that they use the opportunity at the palaver as a way to share their bereavement. They still may be angry with the parent whom they suspect to have brought the disease into their family, and with God for not curing their parents of the illness. The palaver, therefore, provides a safe place for catharsis. Some of those at the palaver might shed a tear, but these moments are for those at the palaver to show their support and to allow the children to grieve and express their emotions.

One of the most important things in this process is for the group to rally around the children and to point out the children's strengths. The fact that these children have been able to survive, or the fact that they may still have some ray of hope, indicates a source of strength. One of the questions to ask the children at the palaver is, what is the source of the strength that sustained you even when the stakes seemed high? Narrative counseling depends on building upon people's strengths rather than their deficits. In addition, it is in the moments of exceptions and mastery experiences described above that one finds the sources of one's strengths. These are moments when one is able to push through, even when the situation is at its toughest. The idea is to tap into those moments of strength and to point toward whatever resources the person was able to use during those dark moments.

Another question asked at the palaver is, are there any stories from the Bible or fairytales or proverbs that have helped you to keep strong, or that you identify with when you are down? In situations where the stories are being misquoted or being used negatively in self-defeat, usually the elder or someone within the group helps identify where the negative application might be happening. This is not for the group to rewrite the person's story, but it is an opportunity for the group to challenge the one telling the story by pointing out how it appears the story is being applied in one's life in a self-defeating manner. This allows the children to "thicken" their story and to be able to see other possibilities and how they might have been narrowly describing their narrative or their life experiences.

Compassion and a Palaver for Widows

When I was on sabbatical in 2003, I asked to go with Mrs. Tsikai (the then United Methodist HIV/AIDS and home-based ministries coordinator) on her home visits with HIV/AIDS patients. I also happened to be teaching a class at United Theological College, Harare, and took advantage of this opportunity for the students to see a hands-on session of what Mrs. Tsikai was doing in this ministry in Epworth, a suburb of Harare. Mrs. Tsikai is also a trained nurse but did this home-based care as her ministry. First, we visited the clinic to see people who were coming for checkups and getting their medicines. After the clinic visit, we then visited those in their homes who were too weak to make the journey to the clinic. In some instances, Mrs. Tsikai told us that it was a matter of days before a patient was going to die. The virus wasted many of the patients' bodies away.

At one house, Mrs. Tsikai introduced us to her patient as pastors and pastors-in-training from the United Theological College. We will call the patient Mrs. Ncube. She was told that we were interested in hearing her story. There were about twelve students with me, and she expressed about how she was so moved emotionally because she had never had so many pastors in her house. She then began to share some of her story, I stopped her, asked permission to have her story recorded, and if I could ask questions as she shared her story. She agreed, and I thanked her for giving me the permission. I also told her that if at anytime she felt she did not want something to be recorded, to let me know.[17]

17. Readers should know that part of the interview was not recorded because we had someone disturbing the interview, who claimed to be the area political-party

Mrs. Ncube's little girl (Patience), who had been raped, was sitting next to her, and Mrs. Tsikai asked her to leave the room since she knew the conversation would involve Patience's story. Tell us your story of what happened, Mrs. Ncube" Mrs. Tsikai asked.[18]

"My work to support the family has been to do odd jobs and selling cloths, etc, in the neighboring rural areas bordering the city. Sometimes I would be gone for periods of two weeks. One day after I came back, my older son said that my little girl was not feeling well and asked if I could take her to the doctors. I checked and she had a high temperature. For a week, she had white stuff coming out and her stomach was bloated. I took her to a clinic and the nurse at the clinic called the police. They took me to jail and they questioned me if I had a boyfriend who could have done this to my little girl. I told them I did not have one and that I did not know who could have done this. They released me, and I took my little girl to the hospital. I was there with her for two days. They told me that my daughter had been raped and that she was HIV/AIDS positive. I asked my daughter whether she knew the person who had done this to her. She said she could recognize him if she saw the person. She also said he used to pass by their [the girl's family's] house but that she had not seen him lately. "I can't understand why someone who knew that they were HIV positive would rape my child.

"To tell you the truth, I can't tell you whether it is from my husband, who died three years ago, or whether it is from my boyfriend that I got the HIV infection. As I said, my husband died three years ago, and the death certificate indicated the cause of death as pneumonia and HIV complications. We had three children at that time aged 11 [boy], 9 [girl] and 2 [girl] did not get tested back then since I did not feel sick—and had always felt strong and in good health. I knew I had to work hard to take care of my children. I would go buy clothing in small quantities, such as children's dresses; sometimes adults' shirts and shoes, and then go trade them in the rural areas bordering Harare. On one of my trips

---

chairperson, saying that we should have asked for permission to come to this particular house (which turned out not to be true). Mrs. Ncube told us later that the man just wanted to see what we were doing, and to see if we had brought her material things such as food so he could come later and ask for it. He interrupted parts of the interview, and after we talked to him, he stood outside for a while listening to what was being talked about, and then he left.

18. Mrs. Ncube (pseudonym) interview by Mrs. Tsikai and Tapiwa N. Mucherera, October 15, 2003, videotape, Epworth Mission, Zimbabwe.

back from my sales last year, I met this man who took an interest in me. He seemed decent, kind, and calm, and I developed a liking of him. I thought, "Here was someone who could make a good husband for me and become a father to my children." The relationship developed, and we became intimate. After we became intimate, he disappeared from my life."

"It also happened that around the time we became intimate, I had started developing a rash on my leg. What I don't remember for sure is whether the rash developed before or after I was intimate with the man. This is the reason why I don't know whether I got the HIV infection from my husband or from this man. I went to the hospital after my leg started swelling up three months later. The results came back, and I was told I was HIV positive."

Mrs. Tsikai told her it was okay to cry if she felt like it. Crying, she continued: "My world fell apart. I thought about my children. Who would care for them? I let down my children. At one point, I had decided to buy *rogga* [poison] and cook it in the food, give it to the little one and myself, and die. The older ones could take care of themselves. I went to a support group at Moving On [an organization with centers where support groups meet]; that helped me see that I needed to be there for my children, and that my family was not worse off than other families since I was still alive. Other children of the same age as mine did not have either of their parents."

Mrs. Tsikai asked her if these thoughts of wanting to kill herself were still with her, to which she responded, "No, right now I am just worried about my little girl."

Mrs. Tsikai also asked Mrs. Ncube what her needs were. She said that mainly it was putting food on the table for her children.

"If I had a helper such as my late husband, things would be much easier for me not to overwork even though I feel ill. Since my leg is so swollen, I can't go to trade anymore, so it has been hard for me to feed the children. I can't walk very far because of my leg." (The leg looked as if she had elephantiasis.) "The church has been helping us. My older boy told his teacher he could not come up with school fees and the teacher helped him."

As a whole group, we collected enough money to pull them through a month or two. Again, she was in tears and thankful of what we were doing for her.

"I felt guilty because I feel responsible for how I contracted HIV. I have never had so many pastors in my house and for you all to want to hear my story as well as contributing so much money has set my heart at peace to say God still cares for me. I have always wanted the church people to hear my story," she finished, crying.

Mrs. Tsikai asked her, "What do you wish for the future, and what gives you hope?"

"What I hope for the future is for my children not to struggle. I hope they take care of themselves—not to catch the HIV disease. I pray that they have a brighter future than mine. It is also people like you who give me hope. Your generosity, and you [Mrs. Tsikai] coming every time to see how I am doing and giving me the medicine I need. Today, you all came to see me; I have never had so many pastors in my house. I believe that this is a sign that God also still loves me and forgives me for my trespasses and sins. I struggled with forgiving myself. I blamed myself for the HIV infection. I did not think I deserved forgiveness since I brought this on myself, and the church would be right to condemn me. Your coming has set me free. My extended family now blames me for all this suffering, saying I brought it on the children and myself. They even suspect that I know the person who raped my little girl. Thank you all for coming and listening to my story."

Mrs. Tsikai showed Mrs. Ncube how to clean her wounds and then gave her some medications. We asked if we could pray for her and her little girl. The little girl, Patience, was called in, and we prayed for both of them. What a palaver. Even though we did not bring a cure to Mrs. Ncube, at the end of the prayer she was filled with so much joy and peace. She told us that even though she did not expect to be *cured* of the HIV infection, this day she had received the *healing* her soul needed and she was freed. Our presence was a confirmation that God still cared for her and that God still loved her.

A Mother's Unconditional Love[19]

In 2004, I was home in Zimbabwe with my mother. She told me that one of our neighbors we were very close to, Mai Madube, had just died of

---

19. In chapter 3, I presented this story about poverty. I reuse it in this chapter to flesh out the details of how the system of the palaver was used to support Mai Madube when she became ill after being infected with HIV while caring for her son.

AIDS. Growing up, I had known both this woman and her husband as a very strong, dedicated Christian couple. When my mother told me she had died of AIDS, my response was, "She couldn't have died of AIDS; they were a very strong Christian couple; one wouldn't expect such from such a couple." My mother looked at me with disbelief. She read my mind. She said, "Even strong Christians with good values are dying of AIDS too, my son. You have been in America too long. You read, see, and believe all the lies they tell you on TV that all people in Africa are dying of AIDS because of extramarital sex and sexual promiscuity. Yes, there are some who are dying because of these affairs, but that is not the whole story. I don't know how many people we have buried so far, who died of HIV/AIDS, who did not engage in these behaviors at all."

She went on to say that Mai Madube had not died of AIDS because she engaged in extramarital affairs; her husband didn't either. "She did not die of AIDS," my mother said, "but died of poverty and a mother's love."

"You see, Mai Madube's son, Tatenda, contracted HIV/AIDS. How? Nobody seems to know. Tatenda had a big open bleeding wound on his foot that would not heal. The mother had to dress this wound every day. Some people told her she would get AIDS because she was touching the open wound with her bare hands. She knew about gloves, but because of poverty, she could not afford to buy gloves. Madube's family had to think of putting food on the table first before they could think about buying gloves. Others even wondered how she had such a stomach not to loathe and be averse to taking care of her son who had a wound that smelled like gangrene—a situation many believed he had brought on himself.

"Mai Madube had vowed that as long as her son lived, she would love him and treat him like a person, and that she did not want him to experience a lonely death because of this horrendous disease. She took care of her son for almost six months, and it is during that time she contracted the disease. She had some blisters that opened up from weeding her garden, and she had continued to take care of Tatenda with those open blisters in her hands. She washed her hands all the time as is the advice, but she still caught the disease. "For us who knew Mai Madube, and have seen this type of thing happening many times, Mai Madube did not die of AIDS, she died of poverty and a mother's love."

My mother went on further to say that at her age of seventy, she had never experienced such death and suffering as she had witnessed in these last two decades. "The person who invented HIV/AIDS will never enter heaven," she said. "This is the genocide of genocides, and he or she knew well to put HIV in poor countries where one can 'smell poverty,' where there is no medicines and/or the necessary material to take care of the infected. I think the person really wanted to wipe out all the poor people from the face of the earth so the rich can then come and take over the lands," she said. When one walks the streets you meet all these young children without parents. Whoever thought a twelve-year-old "with milk still coming out of his nose" could be a head of a household. I pray to the Lord to put a stop to this unnecessary suffering."

I talked to my mother about what had been going on with Mrs. Madube when she became ill after contracting the disease. My mother said that she and her three other friends would go to visit Mrs. Madube almost every week just to sit and talk, and pray with her. They created a palaver for Mrs. Madube. She said they talked about the evils of the illness and the plight of many who were dying alone, especially the widows, and about the issues of poverty. They also talked about how so many people lose friends, church support, and the support of extended family members. Other family members reach the point of saying, "Call me only when he or she is ready for burial." People have seen so much suffering and dying that some try to shield themselves from the pain by choosing not to be involved with those who are dying, something that is totally anticultural to Shona people's values. People never used to die alone. She said, in some of their palavers they took time to pray for those dying alone, those who had lost hope, especially in the Lord, due to their horrendous suffering. The main question with which they wrestled the most was where God was in the midst of all this suffering. They also talked about whether God was punishing their people, "because if God was seeing this, surely God would do something." Interestingly, one of the conclusions they came to was, whether in this life or in death, their lives were still in God's hands. They concluded that from God they came, and to God they would return, even though the return for many was now paved with much suffering. In fact, they had ended at their last palaver with Mrs. Madube on this subject. My mother said she knew that because of their palaver meetings and the spiritual and emotional support they offered to her, Mrs. Madube died at peace in her mind and soul.

Widow Inheritance

I have on video an interview I conducted with a woman (we will call her Mrs. Simango) in her late forties who had just been widowed.[20] The husband, however, did not die of HIV/AIDS; rather he died in an accident. The reason that I use this case is that some of the experiences she went through are similar to those of many widows who are losing their husbands to the HIV/AIDS pandemic. (You might recall the case I cited earlier, of the widow who approached me at a funeral.)

Mrs. Simango and her husband were both trained engineers. The husband was a city engineer in one of the cities. They also owned a company that was operating a very successful business making soap. It so happened that they went on a trip together and when they got back, it dawned on them that they did not have a will. They decided to have a living will drawn up for both of them just in case one of them passed away, or if both of them should die. The will was put in place just a couple years before the husband died. One Saturday Mr. Simango was on top of the roof of his company checking a leak and he fell to the ground. He was taken to the hospital but did not survive. Mr. Simamgo was survived by his wife and his sons (one abroad and the other doing secondary education).

After the burial, the family set a date, as is within the Shona tradition, to distribute the deceased's property. Word got out that the brother of the deceased (a seventh grader by education) with a small plot in a rural area wanted to take over the running of the soap company. The will was brought forth through the lawyer, and it stated that the property was to be left in the hands of the wife. The brother who wanted the company was livid, and wanted to involve a medicine person in the process to get his way, but finally he lost support from some of the elders in the extended family, and he failed. Mrs. Simango stood her ground, and the issue of inheritance was settled according to the will. The downside was that she lost relationships with some of the extended family members

20. Mrs. Simango (pseudonym), interview by Tapiwa N. Mucherera, September 19, 2003, videotape, Mutare, Zimbabwe.

from her deceased husband's side, especially with those who were in support of the older brother who had been vying for the property.

Mrs. Simango was very fortunate that she and her husband had prepared a will before the death of the husband. Even in situations where there is a known will, many widows today suffer because some families do not follow the Western guidelines of the will but instead follow traditional inheritance customs. In these instances where the family chooses the traditional route, the extended family decides who gets what, not based on capabilities, but usually because of their relationship to the deceased (as a brother, sister, or uncle, for example). If they had followed the traditional custom in Mrs. Simango's case, the brother who wanted the company would have easily gotten it even though he did not have the qualifications to run it.

In some situations, if the brother was very much interested in marrying Mrs. Simango as his second wife (wife inheritance), she would be given options, such as getting married to the brother, staying with the family (if she said no to remarrying the brother and also to ever remarrying as long as she was part of the family), or leaving the family and the children behind. This may vary from family to family. In some families where there are strong Christians, and in few traditional families, the widow is usually given the option to choose what is best for her and the children. However, in many families where traditional customs are followed, many widows today are forced to do that which is against their will, unless they have one of the key elders (a man or a woman) in the family defending their wishes. Some widows have been forced into marriages where the surviving brother, interested in the deceased's wife, may be suspected of being HIV infected. In such situations, some women have chosen to leave the family and their children, only to see their children occasionally. The children may end up being abused or may feel orphaned, even though they might still have one parent alive. There are even instances where the children have run away to be with their mother. This traditional system of inheritance needs revision. The purpose of this system in the traditional society was to ensure that the widow would not have to carry the burden of raising her children alone.

These widows need a palaver of their own as well. They need to share about the loss of their husbands, the loss of relationships with extended families, and even the loss of their children if they are forced to move away from the family. Mrs. Simango shared with me how she thought her women's church group would be a fitting place for her to share her struggles—but she found that it was not. The group was a mixture of young married women, middle-aged women, and older widows. Since she was in her early grieving stages, she shared (in tears) with the group how she missed taking time off on Saturday afternoon with her husband, how they would take long showers and massage each other's backs and just relax. As she shared this, one of the older leaders, a widow as well, asked her to be quiet and to spare this "Christian" group all the other details unworthy for them to hear. Mrs. Simango said that she was so embarrassed and shocked by this response, since she had thought that what she was sharing would have been appropriate for an all-women's group. She had thought she could share anything, but, sadly, found this was not the case. She stopped going to the women's fellowship and instead started meeting with a few friends whenever she felt she needed someone with whom to talk. The friends provided her with the "palaver" she needed.

Young widows such as Mrs. Simango desperately need a palaver. They need a place to process their grief and pain without feeling embarrassed. They need a place that is safe, where they can receive unconditional love from people who are nonjudgmental.

Sometimes the situation is worsened when a widow's deceased husband is known or suspected to have died of HIV/AIDS. Often there is loss of relationship with friends, with others treating her as one who is "just waiting for her death," and not as a human being who is still full of life. Many of these young widows have their property stripped away because of greedy and selfish family elders. There are no guidelines encouraging everyone to have a will, and the downside is that in a situation where there is no will, the extended family decides who gets what. Some widows end up withdrawing into themselves, depressed, while others may actually commit suicide. Creating a palaver for people in such situations helps the widows to find a safe place to share and to be cared for.

Besides palaver support groups, some women have organized themselves to start projects of self-support. Some have been given sewing machines or seed money to start projects such as raising chickens or vegetables. Many of these widows, especially in the rural areas, are stay-at-home mothers who depended on the income from their husband's employment in the city. So their new projects help to meet the physical needs of these widows, including those of their family.

The Palaver: A Place to Speak the Unspeakable

A common Shona saying and belief is that silence is golden. I want to challenge this old adage and say there are times when silence is not golden but actually dangerous for the community. In most indigenous contexts today, especially in Zimbabwe, I believe (to paraphrase the biblical book of Esther) that if we keep silent, we will continue to perish (cf. Esth 4:13–14). We are at that point due to the HIV/AIDS pandemic, and we need to speak the unspeakable. The only way for the unspeakable to lose its power is for the unspeakable to be spoken. A priority is to speak the truth about the decay in cultural values in terms of what it means to be a community. In addition, another "unspeakable" that needs to be challenged today is the bad economic structures because of corruption and mismanagement of resources by some of the greedy leaders in power. The unspeakable is also facing the issues of HIV/AIDS in its connection to sex, and even challenging some of the traditional ways of life.

HIV/AIDS touches the two major markers of human life, the beginning and the end in this physical world. The two markers are sex (where conception takes place) and death (the end of the physical life as known by humans). From its discovery, HIV/AIDS has been associated with sex and death, even though there are cases where infection was not directly related to sex. Usually people are not comfortable talking about these two life markers. Even without HIV/AIDS, humanity has always struggled to openly deal with, or talk about, sex and death. Through these two markers, HIV/AIDS is a public threat to humanity; but these markers are usually not given to public debate around the world. World cultures do not know how to fully and publicly embrace these two facts of life, and many world cultures tend to talk about sex and death in casual or flippant ways, or sometimes not at all.

For those who are from the Judeo-Christian tradition, this might not be a surprise. As much as there has been debate about the story of Adam and Eve in the Garden of Eden, and about the type of sin in which they participated, generally, the sin committed is assumed to be that associated with sex. After disobeying God by eating the fruit from the tree, it made them realize they were naked (Gen 3:7, 10). Nakedness is usually associated with sex. In the Scriptures, the punishment that Adam and Eve receive is that of death: "from dust you came, and to dust you shall return" (Gen 3:19). Biblical scholars may not agree with the way I have referenced these passages, and I realize there is more to them than what I have put on paper. But no matter how one may exegete these passages, many of our lay Christian people commonly see these passages as having connotations of sex (nakedness) and thereby as clearly stating the punishment for Adam and Eve's disobedience to be death. Thus, this view of the Genesis story does not surprise me since humanity has always struggled with these two issues. As humans, we are afraid to bring these elements of sex and death from our "subconscious" into our "conscience"; so we avoid addressing them. I am not advocating that people should seek after death, but rather to be able to face it and talk about it when it shows its face. Full-blown AIDS is a death sentence. There are no two ways about it. Why not help a person see the hope beyond the physical death by talking about it openly? Rather than focusing on the physical aspect that is perishing, why not offer them spiritual freedom and love in Christ and the everlasting hope of the life to come?

In the African traditional context, life does not end with physical death, and this is true for African Christians when they read the Scriptures (e.g., John 14:1–21). Our job as caregivers is to engender hope in the dying, to let them know there is life after this life, and to help them prepare for life eternal.

In traditional contexts such as Zimbabwe, sex is not given to public debate. The dilemma is that of the connection between HIV/AIDS and sex. How can we talk about the relationship of sex to HIV/AIDS with our children, and publicly address the problem? Here is my suggestion: Let the palaver be the place for children, young adults, and older adults to come together to educate one another about the disease, about behavior changes needed in the face of HIV/AIDS, and about ways to prevent it. The article below, from a Zimbabwean local newspaper, is also challenging the culture of silence pertaining to the subject of sex.

> Zimbabwe must drop the culture of hushing questions of debates relating to sex. Everyone must talk openly about it so that people understand the advantages and disadvantages related to it.

Destroying this culture will demystify the fantasies and re-dress unequal relations that emanate from cultural ideas. There is limited room for communication because a more equal per-son would not want to listen to the less equal. Becoming AIDS-free does not mean that the virus and those who are infected and affected by it goes away. It means entities, individuals, fami-lies, and communities take steps and organize themselves to encourage behavior-change through activities that stop the transmission of the virus. It also involves taking action to ac-cept and care for those affected by the disease. There is need to create an environment in which people living with AIDS can come out openly and talk about their condition without being discriminated against by society.

Mr. Makaza [a health worker and official] urged people to do away with stigmatization since it stops other people from re-vealing their HIV status. In an interview recently with a female school-going teenager (name disclosed), she says becoming open and talking about one's HIV status is a resounding argu-ment since one can be relieved by discussing his/her problem with others rather than keeping it to one's self. However, the teenager says the problem with it is that of stigmatization. "My sister has once been infected with an STD, and when she ex-plained her problem to friends, they all turned their backs to her saying they do not sympathize with one who risks her life. They no longer regarded her as a friend. Even I, myself, began refusing to share the same bed with my sister because of the fear that I might contract the disease," she said. The teenager says she is now aware of behavior changes she must make and is willing to provide counseling to those infected and affected by the scourge. She now has a positive attitude towards those infected by HIV and AIDS. She encourages people to get tested and know their HIV status.[21]

The saying that prevention is better than cure is true. I share the following common story I have heard to drive the point home.

Prevention Is Better Than a Cure

A group of people was about to cross a river when they saw dead bodies floating down the river and followed by people who were still alive be-ing swept away by the current. They decided to set up a rescue-mission

---

21. Chikomo, "Behavior Change Vital in HIV and AIDS Fight."

station at that point of the river to rescue those who were still alive and to drag out as many of the dead they could so as to accord them proper burial. More people from the community came and helped them to save those who were still alive. A woman came along and started helping in the rescue mission, but as more bodies kept coming, she asked the others where these bodies were coming from. No one seemed to know since they were all focused on rescuing those they could. The woman asked the group if she could have half of the group to go with her up the river to find out why people were ending up in the river in the first place. Half the group stayed at the mission station to rescue those they could, and the rest of the community group went up the river. The woman's idea was to go to the source of the problem and rescue people before they were taken downstream by the current. The rescue-mission station down the river acted as a cure while the woman's idea was prevention at the source of the problem.

One of the prevention approaches in indigenous contexts is that of being able to speak of the traditionally unspeakable. Again, if we keep silent and do not speak, we will surely continue to perish. When one speaks the unspeakable, one usurps it of its control and dominance, thus demystifying its influences. It becomes common. It is understood that once one gives a name to something, the one who does the naming achieves a very high degree of control over the thing. Likewise, speaking the unspeakable helps people to be able to name an oppressive power in order to have some control over it.

In another newspaper article, the author shares how some Zimbabweans are reluctant to talk about HIV, especially with their children. However, those families that are open to talking about it help their children address this issue.

> Wedzerai Chiyoka, the director of Voluntary Services Overseas (VSO), said stigma on HIV/AIDS issues was a result of families' denial to cope with the reality of the pandemic. VSO is a regional organization working with local NGOs involved in HIV/AIDS projects. "More than fifty percent of the Zimbabwean population is still reluctant to discuss HIV/AIDS within their families. Parents do not want to discuss these issues with their children unless a third party is involved," Chiyoka said. She attributed the reluctance to cultural beliefs that view the subject of sex as a taboo.

Chiyoka added that VSO had found that families who spoke openly about HIV/AIDS experienced less stigma and discrimination in the society compared to those who were still reluctant to accept the reality. "Even for children who discuss the subject of HIV/AIDS within their families, it is easier for them to cope when the pandemic affects or infects them," observed Chiyoka.[22]

From a Christian and Jewish perspective, the first thing God did in creating everything was to name that which God was creating (Gen 1:1–31). Not only did God name his creation. God also gave power to humanity to name the rest of his creation. Humanity had the power to name everything from the smallest animals, trees, mountains, and rivers, to diseases. Even the most shunned diseases such as leprosy were given names.

As stated before, the best way to remove stigma is to talk about diseases such as HIV/AIDS using the culturally coined names, and to discuss the diseases in an externalizing fashion.[23] Externalization helps to provide space between the person affected and the problem, leaving room for people to be able to express the usually inexpressible. When the problem is externalized, people are given freedom to step back, be objective, and analyze the problem without feeling blamed. One of the most popular books around the world is from the West, titled *Animal Farm,* and is a good example of externalization.[24] The book uses animals as players to show how political leaders (humans), starting with very good intentions of equality, can let power get to their heads and easily become corrupt. The story hits head-on the sociopolitical problems and injustices in government systems around the world, without pointing fingers to any particular person. The beauty of externalization is that when it is used in stories, people are given room to draw their own conclusions.

On one occasion in his ministry, Jesus used the externalizing approach in talking to Pharisees who bring him a woman caught in adultery (John 8:2–11). They ask Jesus what to do with the woman since in the laws of Moses state that the woman must be stoned to death. Jesus does not respond directly to the fact of whether the woman must be

22. "Zimbabweans Still Reluctant."

23. White and Denborough, *Introducing Narrative Therapy,* 139–47.

24. Orwell, *Animal Farm.*

stoned or left to live. Jesus redirects the focus from the condemnation of the woman as a person to a focus on freedom from the woman's act of adultery (sin). (Interestingly, the question of the whereabouts of the man who had committed the act with the woman was never raised). Jesus's externalizing question with the Pharisees is not whether the woman deserves to die or not, but that anyone among them who has no "sin" (who has never acted sinfully) is invited to cast the first stone. Jesus does not justify the lifestyle but challenges the whole community by externalizing all sinful community behaviors, not just the sin of adultery. In other words, Jesus is also saying that the problem is not "the woman as a person" but sinful acts, including that of adultery committed by the woman. For Christ, the person is not the problem, but rather sin is the problem. In the end, no one could cast a first stone, because everyone had at some level sinned.

Christ saw in the woman a child of God fettered by a sinful act, but the sinful act was not the totality of the woman's identity. As the conversation continues between Christ and the woman, Jesus sees in her a child of God created in the image of God, and he wants to reach out for the re-creation of the distorted image within her. Christ is making a statement to the community that this woman is a beloved human being struggling with sin. At the end of the pericope, he says to the woman, "Woman, where are they? Has no one condemned you? . . . Neither do I condemn you. Go your way, and from now on do not sin again" (John 8:10–11). Jesus sends the woman back to the community, but this time she is a different woman, in that she has been released from the oppressive powers of sin. By externalizing her sin and freeing the woman, Jesus gives the woman a new identity. She has to go back into the same community to meet the same men she had prostituted with, but this time she has a *new identity* that is focused on the honoring of herself in her relationship with God. She is going back to the same family where she will probably be despised and rejected, but with her new self, she will be able to show that she is now different. The woman is still living in the same body but with a different spirit and story. My assumption is that she can talk about her past or share the story of her life with freedom, since her full identity is not wrapped up in the sinful acts of the past. As Jesus treats this woman, we should, likewise, embrace those with no hope, offering each person hope, love, and a new identity in Christ.

The Palaver: Education and Support—Never Go It Alone

One of the main functions of the palaver is to provide people in general a place where they can come and learn in a safe educational environment. Together those who come to the palaver can learn and discuss the dynamics of grief, spiritual questions about God, and how to prevent infection.

The saying among the Shona referred to earlier: "When you find a tortoise sitting on a tree branch, it did not get there by itself." Whether the tortoise wanted to sit on that tree branch or whether it was there by no choice of its own, the tortoise must never forget that it did not get on that tree branch by itself (since a tortoise cannot climb trees). Positively, this saying can be applied to mean that if one finds oneself successful, in a "high-ranking position," one should never forget that one did not get there without the support, prayers, forgiveness, and encouragement of others. If one were to look at one's successes, one would find many people who sacrificed for the person to be sitting on that "tree branch of success." In other words, one never succeeds alone; it takes a company of support or a community for one to be successful. When one realizes the importance of the community, then one is never without hope.

On the other hand, the saying can also be applied when people find themselves "between a rock and a hard place." When we find ourselves in situations that are undesirable, many times it might be because someone did not take time to hold us accountable. This is not to blame the community for all bad choices, but there are many instances when the community watches someone making poor choices and does nothing. In these instances, the community has committed a sin by omission. The community has put one "on a branch of a tree" by neglecting accountability for a person or ignoring a relationship that resulted in woundedness.

It is believed that since people's wounds or pain occurred in the context of relationship or community, it is only out of the context of relationships or community that healing can be achieved. One finds healing in the wisdom of many, and in the support and empathy of others. At the palaver, one can learn from others' wisdom and experiences, and can learn from one's own mistakes, as one is held accountable. One gets the sense that one is not in a given crisis by oneself. When the individual can no longer clearly see or think because the pain is clouding his or her vision, others provide a different perspective on the pain. In other words, when someone is sitting in "a cloud of witnesses" that give voice to the pain, that person is given the freedom to recruit others, or others' stories of strength, for the journey through the crisis. The cloud of witnesses at the palaver becomes one's source of strength during the journey through crisis.

The cloud of witnesses includes those who might have experienced similar pain as well as the spiritual presence of God, and those who are cheering this person on and encouraging him or her not to give up. When one hears similar stories of pain, one becomes strong, hopeful, and optimistic about one's own situation. The palaver creates that space of hope.

Crisis tends to disrupt one's sense of meaning. A palaver provides that place for "meaning making." If one is not aware of grief dynamics, this is one of those places where one can hear and learn the process. They can also learn about how grief affects one's spiritual life and how to make sense out of the chaos created by grief. The palaver helps people rediscover or to identify through interaction with others those strengths that they never knew existed, or that they had simply overlooked. The fact is, life was never created to be lived alone. Humans are creatures of relationships.

Within this chapter I have addressed the holistic approach using narrative counseling. I have shown that the best way to work with or-phaned children is to give them more than emotional (psychological) support—that is, to also be mindful of their physical and spiritual needs. The palaver may not provide the cure for HIV that the world is looking for, but it can surely provide a safe place for healing—relationally, emo-tionally, and spiritually—for the infected and the affected. The same applies to those who want to work with widows in these indigenous contexts such as Zimbabwe. Some of the traditional inheritance cus-toms need to be revised, and there is also need to form support groups for these struggling widows. The palaver is the place for education and support, and for people to be able to speak the unspeakable.

As a whole, this book has addressed the issues of poverty and the HIV/AIDS pandemic as the most difficult problems faced in indig-enous contexts. Poverty combined with poor health systems is causing horrendous suffering in many of the indigenous settings.

Cultural changes due to colonization, Christianity, and urbanization, and the adoption of some Western ethical standards such as confidentiality, corrupt government have exacerbated the problems present in indigenous contexts. However, even in the face of this suffering, many have not lost hope—hope in God and in the family of God found in community.

Bibliography

Agence France Presse. "AIDS Victims 'Buried Alive' in PNG." August 2007. Online: http://www.news.yahoo.com/070828/afp/070828072338asiapacificnews.html.

Akin-Ogundeji, Oladele. "Some Thoughts on the Relevance of Applied Psychology in Africa." *International Journal of Psychology* 22 (1987) 483–91.

Appiah-Kubi, Kofi. "Religion and Healing in an African Community: the Akan of Ghana." In *Healing and Restoring: Health and Medicine in the World's Religious Traditions*, edited by Lawrence E. Sullivan, 203–24. New York: Macmillan, 1989.

Ariarajah, Wesley S. *Gospel and Culture.* Gospel and Cultures Pamphlet 1. Geneva, Switzerland: WCC, 1994.

Armstrong, Robert G., et al. *Socio-political Aspects of the Palaver in Some African Countries.* Paris: UNESCO, 1979.

Associated Press. "AIDS Testing Recommended for Most Americans." Online: http://www.msnbc.msn.com/id/14938109/.

BBC. "Global Aid Failing Poor Nations." February 28, 2005. Online: http://news.bbc.co.uk.

———. "SA Leader Urges Virginity Tests." September 23, 2004. Online: http://news.bbc.co.uk.

Bediako, Kwame. "The Roots of African Theology." *International Bulletin of Missionary Research* 13 (1989) 58–62.

Bell, Catherine. *Ritual Theory, Ritual Practice.* New York: Oxford University Press, 1992.

Berends, William. "African Traditional Healing Practices and the Christian Community." *Missiology: An International Review* 21 (1993) 275–88.

Berinyuu, Abraham Adu. "Change, Ritual and Grief: Continuity and Discontinuity of Pastoral Theology in Ghana." *Journal of Pastoral Care* 46 (1992) 141–52.

———. *Towards Theory and Practice of Pastoral Counseling in Africa.* European University Studies Series XXVII: Asian and African Studies 25. New York: Lang, 1989.

Bourdillon, Michael F. C. *The Shona Peoples: An Ethnography of the Contemporary Shona, with Special Reference to Their Religion.* Gweru, Zimbabwe: Mambo, 1991.

Butler, Joey. "It Really Does Take a Village: Uzumba Orphan Trust Keeps AIDS Orphans in Their Own Homes." Online: http://gbgm-umc.org/programs/aidsafrica/uzumba.stm.

Chikara, Fidelis, and Myrl R. S. Manley. "Psychiatry in Zimbabwe." *Hospital and Community Psychiatry* 42 (1991) 943–47.

Chikomo, Hamunyari. "Behavior Change Vital in HIV and AIDS Fight." *Manica Post*, March 23, 2007.

Chimedza, Paul. "Let's Do SARS Act on HIV, Aids: HIV and Mandatory Testing." *Sunday Mail*, May 21, 2006.

————. "Stigma, Discrimination Dangerous." *Sunday Mail*, November 25, 2007. Online: http://www.sundaymail.co.zw/

Chirimuuta, Richard, and Rosalind Harrison-Chirimuuta. *AIDS, Africa, and Racism*. London: Free Association, 1997.

Chitemba, Brian. "Bread Prices Go Up Again," The Chronicle: Bulawayo, Dec. 14, 2005.

Chuma, Emmanuel. "Woman Hangs Self over Small House." *Bulawayo Chronicle*, June 23, 2006.

Cokesbury. *The Holy Bible Containing the Old and New Testaments: New Revised Standard Version*. Nashville: Holman Bible, 1989.

Corey, Gerald, et al. *Issues and Ethics in the Helping Professions*. 6th edition. Pacific Grove, CA: Brooks/Cole/Thomson Learning, 2003.

Daneel, Marthinus L. "The Encounter between Christianity and Traditional African Culture: Accommodation or Transformation?" *Theological Evangelica* 12 (September 1989) 36–51.

Dodge, Ralph E. *The Unpopular Missionary*. Westwood, NJ: Revell, 1964.

————. "Why Ian Smith Must Fail: Rhodesia Holds the Key to Southern Africa's Future." *Christianity and Crisis* 26 (1966) 267–73.

Dube, Musa W. "*Adinkra!* Four Hearts Joined Together: On Becoming Healing-Teachers of African Indigenous Religion/s in HIV & AIDS Prevention." In *African Women, Religion, and Health: Essays In Honor of Mercy Amba Ewudziwa Oduyoye*, edited by Isabel Apawo Phiri and Sarojini Nadar, 131–56. Maryknoll: Orbis, 2006.

————. *Postcolonial Feminist Interpretation of the Bible*. St. Louis: Chalice, 2000.

Epston, David, and Michael Kingsley White. *Experience, Contradiction, Narrative & Imagination*, edited by Jane Hales. Adelaide, Australia: Dulwich Centre, 1992.

Eron, Joseph B., and Thomas W. Lund. *Narrative Solutions in Brief Therapy*. The Guilford Family Therapy Series. New York: Guilford, 1996.

Fanon, Frantz. *The Wretched of the Earth*. Preface by Jean-Paul Sartre. Translated by Constance Farrington. New York: Grove, 1963.

Foucault, Michel. *Power/Knowledge: Selected Interviews and Other Writings 1972–1977*. Edited and translated by Colin Gordon. New York: Pantheon, 1980.

Freedman Jill, and Gene Combs. *Narrative Therapy: The Social Construction of Preferred Realities*. New York: Norton, 1996.

Freeman, Jennifer C., et al. *Playful Approaches to Serious Problems: Narrative Therapy with Children & their Families*. New York: Norton, 1997.

Freire, Pablo. *Pedagogy of the Oppressed*. Translated by Myra Bergman Ramos. New York: Continuum, 1983.

Furman, Ben, and Tapani Ahola. *Solution Talk: Hosting Therapeutic Conversations*. New York: Norton, 1992.

Gelfand, Michael. *Growing Up in Shona Society: From Birth to Marriage*. Gweru, Zimbabwe: Mambo, 1979.

General Board of Global Ministries of the United Methodist Church. "AIDS In Africa: Heartbreak and Hope." Online: http://gbgm-umc.org/health/aidsafrica/

Gilbert, Laurie. "Zimbabwe: How Can We Help Now?" *Chronicle* (May 2003) 8. St. Luke's United Methodist Church (Highlands Ranch, Colorado). Online: http://www.stlukeshr.com/chronicle/Chronicle2003May.pdf.

Gilligan, Stephen G., and Reese Price. *Therapeutic Conversations*. New York: Norton, 1993.

Glausiusz, Josie. "Why Do So Many Africans Get AIDS?" *Discover* (June 2003) 12.

Goldberg, Michael. *Theology and Narrative: A Critical Introduction*. 1982. Reprint, Eugene, OR: Wipf & Stock, 2001.

Hamutyinei, M. A. *Tsumo Namadimikira*. Gweru, Zimbabwe: Mambo, 1984.

———. *Tsumo-Shumo: Shona Proverbial Lore and Wisdom*. Introduced, translated and explained by Mordikai A. Hamutyinei and Albert B. Plangger. 2nd revised edition. Gweru, Zimbabwe: Mambo, 1987.

Hannan, S. J. *Standard Shona Dictionary*. Revised edition. Gweru, Zimbabwe: Mambo, 1994.

Harrison-Chirimuuta, Rosalind J. "Is AIDS African?" Online: http://way.net/dissonance/aidsafr.html.

Hastings, Adrian. "Mission, Church and State in Southern Africa." *Mission Studies* 2 (1985) 22–32.

Hayes, Sharon. "The Story of Simba the Lion." Unpublished paper, Asbury Theological Seminary, Wilmore, KY, 2004.

Jackson, Helen. *AIDS Africa: Continent in Crisis*. Avondale (Harare), Zimbabwe: Southern Africa AIDS Information Dissemination Service (SAFAIDS), 2002.

James, Richard K., and Burl E. Gilliland. *Crisis Intervention Strategies*. 5th edition. Belmont, CA: Thompson Brooks/Cole, 2004.

Kapenzi, Godfrey Z. *The Clash of Cultures: Christian Missionaries and the Shona of Rhodesia*. Washington DC: University Press of America, 1979.

Lessing, Doris. Foreword. In *An Ill-Fated People: Zimbabwe before and after Rhodes*, by Lawrence Vambe, xiii–xxi. London: Heinemann, 1972.

Levy-Bruhl, Lucien. *Primitive Mentality*. New York: Macmillan, 1923.

Littell, Franklin H. "First They Came for The Jews." *Christian Ethics Today* 3 (1997) 29, Online: http://www.christianethicstoday.com/cetart/index.cfm?fuseaction=Articles.main&ArtID=155.

"The Martyrdom of Fr. Gonçalo da Silveira 1561." In *Rhodesian Tapestry: A History in Needlework*, by the Women's Institutes of Rhodesia, et al. Bulawayo: Books of Rhodesia, 1971. Online: http://www.barbaragoss.net/rhodesiantapestry/bindura.html.

Marett, R. R. *The Threshold of Religion*. 2nd edition, revised and enlarged. New York: Macmillan, 1914

Masamba ma Mpolo, and Daisy Nwachuku, editors. *Pastoral Care and Counseling in Africa Today*. African Pastoral Studies 1. New York: Lang, 1991.

Masamba ma Mpolo, and Wilhelmina Kalu, editors. *The Risks of Growth: Counseling and Pastoral Theology in the African Context*. African Pastoral Studies. Nigeria: Daystar, 1985.

Mbalia, Dorothea D. *John Edgar Wideman: Reclaiming the African Personality*. Selinsgrove, PA: Susquehanna University Press, 1995.

Mbiti, John S. *African Religions and Philosophy.* 2nd revised and enlarged edition. Portsmouth, NH: Heinemann, 1990.

Mbuy, Tata H. "The Need for Pastoral Care of Youth in Africa." *African Ecclesial Review* 38 (1996) 2–10.

McFague, Sallie. *Metaphorical Theology: Models of God in Religious Language.* Philadelphia: Fortress, 1982.

McNamee, Sheila, and Kenneth J. Gergen, editors. *Therapy as Social Construction.* Inquiries in Social Construction Series. London: Sage, 1992.

Médecins Sans Frontières. "As WHO and UNAIDS Call for Global Treatment Scale-Up, MSF Asks: 'Where Will Essential Drugs Come From?'" March 28, 2006. Online: http://www.accessmed-msf.org.

Memmi, Albert. *The Colonizer and the Colonized.* Foreword by Jean-Paul Sartre. Afterword by Susan Gilson Miller. Translated by Howard Greenfield. Boston: Beacon, 1991.

Ministry of State Enterprises, Anti-Corruption and Anti-Monopolies. "Fight Corruption." Online: http://www.fightcorruption.gov.zw .

Monk, Gerald. "How Narrative Therapy Works." In *Narrative Therapy in Practice: The Archaeology of Hope*, edited by Gerald Monk, et al., 3–31. San Francisco: Jossey-Bass, 1997.

Morgan, Alice. *What is Narrative Therapy?: An Easy to Read Introduction.* Adelaide, Australia: Dulwich Centre, 2000.

Moyo, Abiot. "Mission Team Returns from Zimbabwe." August 31, 2005. Online: http://www.neumc.org/news_print.asp?PKValue=78/.

Moyo, Ambrose. *Zimbabwe: The Risk of Incarnation.* Gospel and Cultures Pamphlet 8. Geneva, Switzerland: WCC, 1996.

Muchapera, Stewart. "World Vision Launches Urban School Feeding Program." November 11, 2003. Online: http://www.worldvision.org/worldvision/comms .nsf/stable/safc_schoolfeeding/.

Mucherera, Tapiwa N. "Hope in the Midst of Struggle: Church and Parents Together in Raising Teens." In *Keep It Real: Working with Today's Black Youth*, edited by Anne Streaty Wimberly, 83–100. Nashville: Abingdon, 2005.

———. "Narrative Counseling from Non-western Perspective." In *Therapeutic Conversations 5: Therapy from the Outside In*, edited by Stephen Madigan, 18–28. Vancouver, BC: Yaletown Family Therapy, 2004.

———. *Pastoral Care from a Third World Perspective: A Pastoral Theology of Care for the Urban Contemporary Shona in Zimbabwe.* New York: Lang, 2005.

Mulemfo, Mukanda Mabonso. "Palaver as a Dimension of Communal Solidarity in Zaire: A Missiological Study on Transgression and Reconciliation." *Missionalia* 24 (1996) 129–47.

Mungazi, Dickson. *Colonial Education for Africans: George Stark's Policy in Zimbabwe.* New York: Praeger, 1991.

———. *Colonial Policy and Conflict in Zimbabwe: A Study of Cultures in Collision, 1890–1979.* New York: Crane Russak, 1992.

———. *The Mind of Black Africa.* London: Praeger, 1997.

"Murewa Elders Call for Virginity Testing." *Sunday Mail*, November 25, 2007. Online: www.sundaymail.co.zw.

Murphree, Marshall W. *Christianity and the Shona.* London School of Economics. Monographs on Social Anthropology 36. New York: Humanities, 1969.

Musodza R., and Chitiyo, P. "Uzumba Orphan Trust: Report for the Period of 1998–1999." Chitembe, Zambia: 1999.

Musopole, Augustine C. *Being Human in Africa: Toward an African Christian Anthropology.* American University Studies. Series XI, Anthropology and Sociology 65. New York: Lang, 1994.

Mutswairo, Solomon Manguiro, et al. *Introduction to Shona Culture.* Kadoma, Zimbabwe: Juta, Zimbabwe, 1996.

Mutukudzi, Oliver. "Sandi Bonde." *Paivepo,* compact disc. New York: Putumayo World Artists, 2000.

Nandi, Ashis. *The Intimate Enemy: Loss and Recovery of Self Under Colonialism.* Delhi: Oxford University Press, 1983.

Ncube, Mrs. (pseudonym). Interview by Mrs. Tsikai and Tapiwa N. Mucherera. October 15, 2003, videotape, Epworth Mission, Zimbabwe.

Ngugi wa Thiong'o. *Decolonizing the Mind: The Politics of Language in African Literature.* Reprint, Harare: Zimbabwe Publishing House, 1994.

———. *Moving the Centre: The Struggle for Cultural Freedoms.* Portsmouth, NH: Heinemann, 1993.

Nhiwatiwa, Eben K. *Humble Beginnings: A Brief History of the United Methodist Church Zimbabwe: Gleanings from the Heritage of the United Methodist Church in Zimbabwe, Celebrating the Centennial, 1997.* Zimbabwe: n. p. 1997.

"No to Abuse of Power." *The Herald* (Harare), July 15, 2006, front page.

Oduyoye, Mercy. "The Value of African Religious Beliefs and Practices for Christian Theology." In *African Theology En Route: Papers from the Pan African Conference of Third World Theologians, December 17–23, 1977, Accra, Ghana,* edited by Kofi Appiah-Kubi and Sergio Torres, 109–16. Maryknoll: Orbis, 1979.

Orwell, George. *Animal Farm.* Middlesex, England: Harcourt Brace, 1946.

Parry, Alan, and Robert E. Doan. *Story Re-Visions: Narrative Therapy in the Postmodern World.* New York: Guilford, 1994.

Pearce, Stephen S. *Flash of Insight: Metaphor and Narrative in Therapy.* Boston: Allyn & Bacon, 1996.

Phiri, Isabel Aapwo. "Virginity Testing? African Women Seeking Resources to Combat HIV/AIDS." Unpublished paper, University of KwaZulu, Natal (Pietermaritzburg), South Africa, 2003.

PlusNews. "ZIMBABWE: AIDS Orphans and Vulnerable Children Bear the Brunt of Collapsing Economy." Online: http://www.plusnews.org/Report.aspx?ReportId =39161.

Pobee, John. *Toward an African Theology.* Nashville: Abingdon, 1979.

Rukuni, Charles. "Forget about Hunger, Zimbabweans Just Love Sex." *Financial Gazette,* November 29, 2006.

Shotter, John. *Conversational Realities: Constructing Life through Language.* Inquiries in Social Construction. London: Sage, 1993.

Shropshire, Denys W. T. *The Church and the Primitive Peoples.* London: SPCK 1938.

Simango, Mrs. (pseudonym). Interview by Tapiwa N. Mucherera, September 19, 2003, videotape, Mutare, Zimbabwe.

"'Small House' Killed." *Daily Mirror Reporter.* February 24, 2006.

Smith, Archie. *Navigating the Deep River: Spirituality in African American Families.* Cleveland: United Church Press, 1997.

Smith, Craig, and David Nylund, editors. *Narrative Therapies with Children and Adolescents.* New York: Guilford, 1997.

Somé, Malidoma Patrice. *The Healing Wisdom of Africa: Finding Life Purpose through Nature, Ritual, and Community.* New York: Tarcher/Putnam, 1998.

Taylor, Daniel. *The Healing Power of Stories: Creating Yourself through the Stories of Your Life.* New York: Doubleday, 1996.

Tinker, George E. *Missionary Conquest: the Gospel and Native American Cultural Genocide.* Minneapolis: Fortress, 1993

Unendoro, Benedict. "Zimbabwean Students Driven to Prostitution." January 19, 2006. Institute for War & Peace Reporting. January 19, 2006. Online: http://www.iwpr.net.

Vickers, Steve. "Staging Sex Myths to Save Zimbabwe's Girls." BBC. October 24, 2006. Online: http://news.bbc.co.uk/2/hi/africa/6076758.stm.

Whidborne, Vicki A. "Africanisation of Christianity in Zimbabwe." *Religion in Southern Africa* 4 (1983) 31–50.

White, Cheryl, and David Denborough, compilers. *Introducing Narrative Therapy: A Collection of Practice-Based Writings.* Adelaide, Australia: Dulwich Centre, 1998.

White, Michael Kingsley. *Michael White: Selected Papers.* Adelaide, Australia: Dulwich Centre, 1989.

———. *Re-Authoring Lives: Interviews & Essays.* Adelaide, Australia: Dulwich Centre, 1995.

White, Michael Kingsley, and David Epston. *Narrative Means to Therapeutic Ends.* A Norton Professional Book. New York: Norton, 1990.

White, William R. *Speaking in Stories: Resources for Christian Storytellers.* Minneapolis: Augsburg, 1982.

Wicks, Robert J., and Barry K. Estadt, editors. *Pastoral Counseling in a Global Church: Voices from the Field.* Maryknoll: Orbis, 1993.

Williams, Patrick, and Laura Chrisman, editors. *Colonial Discourse and Post-Colonial Theory: A Reader.* New York: Columbia University Press, 1994.

Willowghby, William Charles. *The Soul of the Bantu.* Garden City: Doubleday, 1928.

Wilson, David J., and Susan Lavelle. "Loneliness and General Psychological Distress among Zimbabwean Students." *Journal of Social Psychology* 130 (1990) 273–75.

Wimberly, Edward P. *Recalling Our Own Stories: Spiritual Renewal for Religious Caregivers.* The Jossey-Bass Religion-In-Practice Series. San Francisco: Jossey-Bass, 1997.

———. *Using Scripture in Pastoral Counseling.* Nashville: Abingdon, 1994.

Wimberly, Edward P., and Tapiwa N. Mucherera. "Re-Villaging, Crisis Theory, and the African Context." Paper presented at the fourth Congress of the African Association of Pastoral Studies and Counseling in Yaounde, Cameroon, July 27, 2001.

"Woman Strips 'Small House.'" *Victoria Falls Reporter*, April 8, 2006.

Women's Institutes of Rhodesia, et al. *Rhodesian Tapestry: A History in Needlework.* Bulawayo: Books of Rhodesia, 1971. Online: http://www.barbaragoss.com/rhodesiantapestry/.

"Zimbabweans Still Reluctant to Discuss the HIV and AIDS Issues." *Daily Mirror*, June 28, 2006.

Zimmerman, Jeffrey L., and Victoria C. Dickerson. *If Problems Talked: Narrative Therapy in Action*. The Guilford Family Therapy Series. New York: Guilford, 1996.

ZimOnline. "Girl-Children Sacrificed into Marriage as Hunger Bites in Zimbabwe," May 16, 2006. Online: http://www.zimonline.co.za. Reprinted in: *Mail & Guardian Online* (South Africa). http://www.mg.co.za.

"ZOE Feeding Projects: (Offering Porridge, Mahewu (nutritional drink) and Holiday Food Packs.)" Online: http://www.zoeministry.org/update/feeding_projects.php.

CPSIA information can be obtained at www.ICGtesting.com
Printed in the USA
LVOW08s1111210814

400260LV00003B/161/P